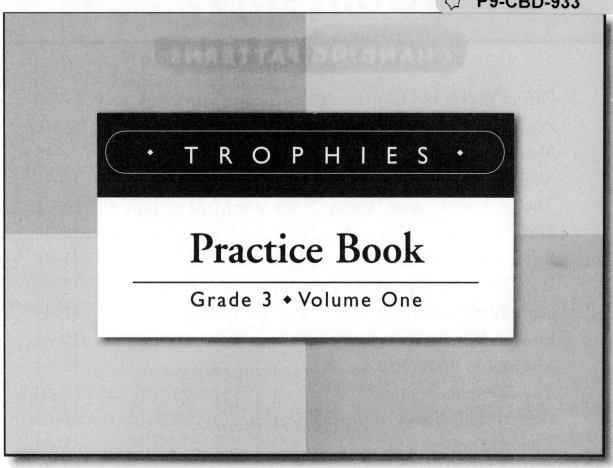

· T R O P H I E S ·

Practice Book

Grade 3 ◆ Volume One

Harcourt

Orlando   Boston   Dallas   Chicago   San Diego

Visit *The Learning Site!*
www.harcourtschool.com

Printed in the United States of America

ISBN 0-15-323516-0

9 10 054 10 09 08 07 06 05 04

Contents

CHANGING PATTERNS

▶ **Read the groups of words on the posters. Write the Vocabulary Word that fits with each group.**

department	obeys	commands	audience
expression	accident	noticed	

1. watchers
listeners
viewers

_____

2. feeling
emotion
looks

_____

3. saw
took note of
observed

_____

4. mistake
error
bad luck

_____

5. directions
orders
strong requests

_____

6. group
section
company

_____

7–8. Complete this safety tip with Vocabulary Words.

The person who _____ traffic rules

is not likely to have an _____.

TRY THIS! Make a poster with safety tips for your classroom.

Name _____

▶ **Read the paragraph and look at the underlined words. Write each word in the correct column below. Then divide each word into syllables.**

I have a talking moose named Charlie. Charlie can be a handful of trouble sometimes. On Tuesday, Charlie wanted to go to school with me. I had to read a report on safety that day in the school auditorium. A police officer would be speaking as well. It was not a good day to bring Charlie to school. I tried to explain this to him, but he wouldn't listen. I asked my mom to write a letter to Charlie asking him to stay at home. She did. It read, "Dear Charlie, I need your help today with the groceries. Love, Mom." I thought that would do it. I used a thumbtack to tack the letter to the message board in my room so that Charlie could read it. He did. Then he ate the letter. So, Charlie came to school with me and helped me read my report. Everyone loved him. I got an A. I guess it turned out better than I thought it would.

VCCV Patterns with Double Consonants	Compound Words	Words with Suffixes or -ed, -ing
pudding pud–ding	someone some–one	asking ask–ing
1. _____ _____	4. _____ _____	7. _____ _____
2. _____ _____	5. _____ _____	8. _____ _____
3. _____ _____	6. _____ _____	9. _____ _____

SCHOOL-HOME CONNECTION Work with your child to divide the Vocabulary Words on page 1 into syllables.

2

Practice Book
Changing Patterns

© Harcourt

Name _____

Skill Reminder • A sentence is a group of words that tells a complete thought.
• The words are in an order that makes sense.
• Begin every sentence with a capital letter, and end it with an end mark.

▶ Rewrite each group of words in the correct order to form a sentence that makes sense. Begin and end each sentence correctly.

1. Officer Buckle welcomed we. _____

2. why a dog bring he did? _____

3. a helmet he always wears. _____

4. buckle your did you seatbelt? _____

5. a letter the students wrote. _____

▶ If the words form a sentence, write *sentence*. If they do not, think of words to make the thought complete. Then write the new sentence.

6. Officer Buckle _____

7. Talked to children about safety. _____

8. Showed the safe way to cross the street.

_____

9. Did the students look both ways when they crossed the street?

_____

10. The students thank Officer Buckle._____

TRY THIS! Write two safety tips for your classroom. Be sure each tip forms a sentence.

Practice Book
Changing Patterns

Officer Buckle
and Gloria

Spelling:
Words with Short a
and Short e

Skill Reminder **You can spell the short _a_ sound with an _a_ and the short _e_ sound with an _e_.**

▶ Fold the paper along the dotted line. As each spelling word is read aloud, write it in the blank. Then unfold your paper, and check your work. Practice spelling any words you missed.

1. _____

2. _____

3. _____

4. _____

5. _____

6. _____

7. _____

8. _____

9. _____

10. _____

11. _____

12. _____

13. _____

14. _____

15. _____

SPELLING WORDS

1. sat
2. felt
3. last
4. send
5. next
6. best
7. went
8. hand
9. stand
10. past
11. grand
12. stamp
13. belt
14. lend
15. checked

© Harcourt

Practice Book
Changing Patterns

▶ **Write the Vocabulary Word that best completes each sentence.**

grumble exploded languages mumbled streak stubborn darted

1. Jack was so upset he could not stand still. He _____ from room to room looking for his Spanish textbook.

2. "Whoever hid that textbook did a good job," Jack

_____ to himself.

3. Jack's sister Gloria heard a low, annoyed sound. She knew the

_____ came from Jack when she saw his face.

4. Gloria also knew Jack would not give up looking. He was the most

_____ person in the family.

5. Jack never wanted to learn any other _____.

6. Jack looked upstairs, downstairs, indoors, and outdoors until he lost

his temper and _____. "WHERE IS MY BOOK?" he yelled.

7. Jack was so loud that he made his cat, Romeo, _____ like a rocket up the stairs. Gloria nearly tripped over poor Romeo as she came out of Jack's room and went downstairs. She was smiling. "Busca en tu pupitre, Jack!" she said. Before Jack could ask any questions, Gloria grabbed her Spanish dictionary and left the house.

TRY THIS! Make a list of all the foreign languages you can think of. Can you add words from any of those languages to your list? If so, write them on the line next to the language(s).

Practice Book
Changing Patterns

© Harcourt

▶ **Read the following passage. Then answer the questions.**

> Matt and Curtis stood in front of the bike rack after school. They decided to bike to Curtis's house. As they reached for their helmets, Matt noticed something was wrong with his. "Oh, no," he said, "the strap's broken. I won't be able to go."
>
> Curtis said, "My house is only two blocks away. You don't need your helmet." Matt thought about what to do.

1. Who are the characters in the story?

_____

2. What is the setting of the story?

_____

3. What is Matt's problem?

_____

_____

4. Why does Curtis think Matt doesn't need his helmet?

_____

_____

5. Why do you think Matt has to think about what to do?

_____

6. How do you think Matt will solve his problem?

_____

© Harcourt

Name _____

▶ **Read the diary entry. Then circle the letter of the best answer to each question.**

Dear Diary,

Today my kitten, Gatito, jumped out of my arms and chased a mouse into the street. My cousin, Juan, was riding his bicycle down the street. He was heading straight for Gatito. "John! Stop!" I yelled. Juan did not stop, because he did not understand English. Then I yelled, "¡Juan! ¡Pare!" Just in time, Juan turned his bike to the right. "Rosa, at first I didn't know you were talking to me," Juan said to me in Spanish. I am lucky that I speak Spanish and English.

Rosa

1 Where does the story take place?

   A at the store

   B in a garden

   C in the forest

   D on a street

> **Tip**
> What words help you tell where the action happens?

2 Who is the main character in the story?

   F Rosa

   G Gatito

   H Juan

   J the bicycle

> **Tip**
> Remember that the main character is usually the one who has a problem to solve.

3 Why does Juan keep riding, even after Rosa shouts out to him?

   A She speaks English, but Gatito understands only Spanish.

   B Rosa speaks to Juan in English, and Juan understands only Spanish.

   C She speaks Spanish, but Juan speaks English.

   D Gatito speaks Spanish, and Juan speaks Spanish.

> **Tip**
> Think about what happens in the story. How are Spanish words used to solve Rosa's problem?

© Harcourt

SCHOOL-HOME CONNECTION With your child, recall a favorite story. Discuss the characters, setting, and plot..

Practice Book
Changing Patterns

Name _____

▶ **Look at the dictionary pages. Then answer the questions below.**

south • squid

south (south) *noun*—A direction on a compass or a map. Opposite of north. abbreviation—S

speak (spēk) *verb*—To say words.

special (spesh′əl) *adjective*—Different or unusual.

spider (spī′dər) *noun*—A small animal with eight legs and no wings. plural—spiders

squid (skwid) *noun*—A sea animal with a long, soft body and 10 tentacles. plural—squid or squids

530

squishy • submarine

squishy (skwish′-ē) *adjective*—Soggy.

still (stil) *adjective*—Not moving or making a noise.

stranger (strān′jər) *noun*—Someone you do not know. plural—strangers

street (strēt) *noun*—A road in a city or a town, usually with sidewalks and buildings along it. abbreviation—St.

submarine (sub•mə•rēn′) *noun*—A ship that can travel underwater. plural—submarines

531

1. Which of the following might be described as *squishy*—oatmeal, rocks, or pencils? _____

2. What is the abbreviation for the word *street?* _____

3. Why are *south* and *squid* shown at the top of page 530?

_____

4. Which words would the word *stingray* go between?

_____

5. What is the plural form of the word *squid?* _____

6. Which of the words is a verb? _____

7. What two things on these pages could you find underwater?

_____

8

Practice Book
Changing Patterns

© Harcourt

Name _____

Skill Reminder • **A statement** is a sentence that tells something. Use a period (.) to end a statement.
• **A question** is a sentence that asks something. Use a question mark (?) to end a question.

▶ After each sentence, write *statement* or *question* to tell what kind of sentence it is.

1. What is the name of your dog?

   _____

2. I am teaching my old dog new tricks.

   _____

3. I like the new student.

   _____

4. Can you sing songs in Spanish? _____

5. I speak two languages. _____

▶ Add the correct end mark to each sentence.

6. Dara speaks English and Spanish —

7. Does she teach English to her little brother —

8. Is he studying English in school —

9. At night he dreams in Spanish —

10. Do you like to sing in Spanish —

 TRY THIS! Read sentences 6–10 aloud. Turn the statements into questions and the questions into statements.

Practice Book
Changing Patterns

© Harcourt

Skill Reminder You can spell the short *i* sound *i*, the short *o* sound *o*, and the short *u* sound *u*.

▶ Fold the paper along the dotted line. As each spelling word is read aloud, write it in the blank. Then unfold your paper, and check your work. Practice spelling any words you missed.

1. _____

2. _____

3. _____

4. _____

5. _____

6. _____

7. _____

8. _____

9. _____

10. _____

11. _____

12. _____

13. _____

14. _____

15. _____

SPELLING WORDS

1. slip
2. fish
3. pick
4. rocks
5. lunch
6. gift
7. thing
8. inch
9. truck
10. pond
11. from
12. jump
13. socks
14. dish
15. thump

Practice Book
Changing Patterns

Name _____

▶ **Write the Vocabulary Word that best completes each sentence.**

case	specific	assistant	definitely
detective	returned	positive	

1. Duncan hires a _____ to solve the mystery of the missing joke book.

2. The book is missing for sure. It is _____ gone.

3. When Nate takes the _____, he begins to study the mystery.

4. An expert like Nate might have a helper

called an _____.

5. Duncan does not want just any joke book. He has a

_____ joke book in mind.

6. Duncan is uncertain about where he left the book. On the other

hand, Nate is _____ it is in the freezer.

7. When Nate _____ the book to Duncan,
he put it back where it belonged.

▶ **Complete the story using the Vocabulary Words.**

Muriel Morgan was the greatest **(8)** _____ in the

third grade. She could solve any **(9)** _____. She was

(10) _____ that she could solve the Mystery of the

Missing Chalkboard Eraser. It was **(11)** _____ the
hardest mystery she had ever worked on. She followed a trail of chalk dust
to Slim Sneaky's desk. Muriel found the eraser in the desk

and **(12)** _____ it to the teacher.

11

Name _____

HOMEWORK

Nate the Great,
San Francisco
Detective

**Decode Long
Words**
TEST PREP

▶ **Read the following newspaper story. Then answer each question below.**

Calvin Cooper Solves Case of the Missing Library Book

San Francisco, January 24—Calvin Cooper solved yet another mystery today. C.C., as his friends call him, found Ashley Johnson's library book. The book was called *Ralph and the Flying Doghouse*. It had been missing for two days. Last Wednesday, C.C. found Ashley sobbing in the hall. "If I do not return my book, I will not be able to take out another one!" she cried. They looked everywhere. Finally, the trail of clues led C.C. to the library. There, behind a chair, was the book. "It must have dropped out of my backpack!" Ashley exclaimed.

1 Which correctly divides the word *sobbing* into syllables?

   A s–obbing   **C** sob–bing

   B so–bbing   **D** sobbin–g

Tip
Try saying the word aloud. Where does it divide?

2 Which correctly divides the word *return* into syllables?

   F ret–urn   **H** r–eturn

   G re–turn   **J** retur–n

Tip
Ignore answers that do not sound or look right.

3 What are the two shorter words that make up the word *everywhere*?

   A *very* and *here*   **C** *eve* and *her*

   B *ever* and *he*   **D** *every* and *where*

Tip
The word *everywhere* means "in all places."

4 If the word *house* means "a building to live in," then what does the word *doghouse* mean?

_____

_____

SCHOOL-HOME CONNECTION With your child, find three words with two or more syllables in the story above. Work together to divide the words into syllables.

12

© Harcourt

Name _____

▶ **Write the word that describes the literary form.**

| play | newspaper article | poem | fantasy story | biography |

I like you,
And you like me.
We are happy
As can be!

_____

Sir Arthur Conan Doyle wrote detective stories. His most famous character is Sherlock Holmes. Doyle was a doctor before he became a writer.

_____

Jewel Robbery Solved

London, November 3—
The police discovered the hiding place where three robbers hid the jewels. An unknown caller tipped off the police...

_____

Once upon a time, there lived a fearless detective. With the help of her faithful dog, Sleuth, she solved the mystery of the princess's missing crown. Her reward was a castle of her own. There, she and Sleuth lived happily ever after.

_____

Scene 1

Mystery Mike: Tell me where you have buried the loot!

Roberta the Robber: Never! You'll have to catch me first! (*She runs away.*)

Mystery Mike: Ah! Foiled again, isn't that right, Fido?

Fido: Arf!

_____

SCHOOL-HOME CONNECTION Work with your child to find examples of three literary forms. Examples are a newspaper article, a poem, and a fantasy story.

13

© Harcourt

Name _____

Nate the Great,
San Francisco
Detective

Grammar:
Commands and
Exclamations

Skill Reminder • **A command** is a sentence that gives an order or a direction. End a command with a period (.).
• **An exclamation** is a sentence that shows strong feeling. End an exclamation with an exclamation point (!).

▶ Write *command* or *exclamation* to tell what kind of sentence each is. Add the correct end mark to each sentence.

1. What a great detective Nate is __ _____

2. Oops, I spilled the syrup __ _____

3. Search that garbage can, Sludge __ _____

4. Wow, this is a hard case to solve __ _____

5. Meet me at the bookstore __ _____

6. Look on the shelf for the missing book __ _____

▶ Use each word in parentheses ( ) in a complete sentence. For C, write a command. For E, write an exclamation.

7. (house) C: _____

8. (yes) E: _____

9. (help) C: _____

10. (found) E: _____

11. (bookstore) C: _____

TRY THIS! Write four sentences of conversation using exclamations and commands.

Practice Book
Changing Patterns

© Harcourt

Nate the Great,
San Francisco
Detective

Spelling: Words
with Long *a* and
Long *e*

Skill Reminder **You can spell the long e sound
ee or *ea*.**

▶ Fold the paper along the dotted line. As each
spelling word is read aloud, write it in the
blank. Then unfold your paper, and check
your work. Practice spelling any words
you missed.

1. _____

2. _____

3. _____

4. _____

5. _____

6. _____

7. _____

8. _____

9. _____

10. _____

11. _____

12. _____

13. _____

14. _____

15. _____

SPELLING WORDS

1. easy
2. grade
3. meet
4. late
5. seat
6. saved
7. pail
8. these
9. reach
10. name
11. raise
12. leave
13. gain
14. theme
15. scream

Practice Book
Changing Patterns

Name _____

▶ **Write the Vocabulary Word that best completes each sentence.**

| aimed | captain | monitor | pretended | professional | familiar |

1. If you've played a game many times it is a

   _____ game to you.

2. If you acted as if you were a famous

   basketball player, you _____.

3. If you took care of a playground,

   you were probably the park _____.

4. If you want to have a job playing basketball when you grow up, you

   want to be a _____ player.

5. If you tossed the ball toward the basket, you

   _____ it.

6. If you were in charge of your team, you were the team's

   _____.

▶ **Write the Vocabulary Word that fits best with each word or phrase below.**

7. pointed at _____

8. acted _____

 TRY THIS! Write two sentences about your favorite athlete. Use as many of the Vocabulary Words as you can.

16

© Harcourt

Name _____

▶ **Read the paragraph. Then circle the letter of the best answer to each question.**

Alonzo was very small for his age. He wanted to play guitar. Even his older brother, Miguel, made fun of him. "You're a baby, and your hands are too small," Miguel said. "My hands are not too small. I'm going to play guitar," Alonzo replied. Every day after school, Alonzo practiced and practiced. In the beginning, his fingers could barely pluck a single string. Then, one day Alonzo picked up the guitar and strummed a chord. Soon he was playing songs. Miguel couldn't believe it. "I'm sorry for what I said. I was wrong, little brother," Miguel told Alonzo. Alonzo forgot about the teasing and gave Miguel a big hug.

1 What action shows that Alonzo is determined?
  A He practices guitar every day after school.
  B He wants to play guitar.
  C Miguel makes fun of him.
  D He is small for his age.

💡 **Tip**
Think about what Alonzo decides to do.

2 How can you tell that Miguel can be unkind?
  F Miguel said, "I was wrong."
  G Miguel couldn't believe how well Alonzo played guitar.
  H Miguel said to Alonzo, "You are small for your age."
  J Miguel made fun of Alonzo.

💡 **Tip**
What does Miguel do that would make you feel he is being mean?

3 How do you know that Alonzo is a good sport as well as a good guitar player?
  A Miguel teases Alonzo.
  B Alonzo likes to play his guitar.
  C Alonzo gives Miguel a hug.
  D Miguel apologizes to Alonzo.

💡 **Tip**
The question asks about Alonzo, not Miguel.

© Harcourt

SCHOOL-HOME CONNECTION With your child, think about a favorite character from a cartoon or book. Picture something the character does. Describe how the character feels and how he or she shows that feeling.

17

Name _____

Skill Reminder A **subject** tells who or what a sentence is about. A **predicate** tells what a subject is or does.

▶ **Draw one line under each subject. Draw two lines under each predicate.**

1. Allie's friends played in the park.

2. One small girl jumped rope.

3. Julio whizzed by on his skateboard.

4. The park is a wonderful place.

5. Allie feels happy there.

▶ **Add a subject or a predicate to complete each sentence.**

6. The basketball _____.

7. _____ played with a volleyball.

8. _____ watched the game.

9. Some boys _____.

10. _____ cheered for Allie.

 TRY THIS! Write three sentences about playing a game. In each sentence, draw one line under the subject. Draw two lines under the predicate.

Name _____

Skill Reminder   You can spell the long *i* sound *i-e* or *igh*.
You can spell the long *o* sound *o-e* or *ow*.

▶ Fold the paper along the dotted line. As each spelling word is read aloud, write it in the blank. Then unfold your paper, and check your work. Practice spelling any words you missed.

SPELLING WORDS

1. tight
2. while
3. show
4. stone
5. bright
6. whole
7. window
8. time
9. follow
10. close
11. flight
12. tide
13. grow
14. broke
15. below

1. _____

2. _____

3. _____

4. _____

5. _____

6. _____

7. _____

8. _____

9. _____

10. _____

11. _____

12. _____

13. _____

14. _____

15. _____

© Harcourt

Practice Book
Changing Patterns

Name _____

▶ **Write the Vocabulary Word that best completes each sentence.**

| ceremonies | ancient | compete | host |
| earned | stadium | medals | record |

1. Rodney is going to _____ in the third-grade whistling contest.

2. His class is going to be the _____ of the event.

3. He helped put up a sign over the classroom door that says: Welcome

to Whistling _____.

4. _____ are awarded for the loudest whistle, the longest whistle, and the prettiest whistle.

5. The current school _____ for the longest whistle is held by "Screeching" Maxine Jackson.

6. The school band plays at the opening

_____.

7. Following _____ tradition, the whistling athletes drink lemonade before the contest begins.

8. Rodney told Maxine that she _____ her victory by practicing hard.

 TRY THIS! Make up an unusual Olympic sport. Use three of the Vocabulary Words to write a description of the sport.

© Harcourt

Practice Book
Changing Patterns

Name _____

▶ **Read the paragraph. Then circle the letter of the best answer to each question.**

U.S. runner Marion Jones is one of the world's greatest runners. The story of her life shows how hard work and determination can make a dream come true. Marion had wanted to compete in the Olympics ever since she was a child. She trained every day to build up her speed and strength. Marion Jones fulfilled her dream in the year 2000. She won three gold medals and two bronze medals at the Olympic Games in Sydney, Australia.

1 The paragraph could be from
   A a biography.
   B a folktale.
   C a how-to article.
   D a school newsletter.

> 💡 **Tip**
> Where would you most likely find information about a famous person?

2 This paragraph is nonfiction because
   F the author admires Marion Jones.
   G Marion Jones is famous.
   H it tells about a real person and gives information.
   J it is interesting to read.

> 💡 **Tip**
> Remember that nonfiction is based on facts.

3 Where would you NOT find this paragraph?
   A in an informational book about running
   B in a magazine article about the Olympic Games
   C in a news story about Marion Jones
   D in a mystery story

> 💡 **Tip**
> Which type of writing does not have to tell about real life?

Practice Book
Changing Patterns

Name _____

▶ **Write the type of nonfiction from the box that best matches each description.**

news story	**newsletter**	**magazine article**
how-to article	**biography**	**informational book**

1. an article about Marion Jones that is part of a publication with other articles, photographs, and advertisements

   _____

2. an article about becoming a faster runner

   _____

3. a history book about the Olympics

   _____

4. a story telling that Marion Jones just won five gold medals

   _____

5. an article about sports at your school

   _____

6. a book that tells the story of Marion Jones's life

   _____

▶ **Answer the questions below.**

7. Give two reasons why a biography of Marion Jones is called nonfiction.

   _____

8. Why is a story about a girl who can fly called fiction?

   _____

© Harcourt

SCHOOL-HOME CONNECTION With your child, look at some nonfiction reading materials, such as newspapers, magazines, and reference books. Discuss how they are different from fiction.

22

Practice Book
Changing Patterns

▶ **Read the paragraphs and answer the questions.**

Olympic Dream Comes True

The crowd cheers when Connie twirls and jumps across the ice. She knows her performance is perfect so far. Now is the time for the final jump. Connie knows this is the big moment.

1. What is Connie doing? _____

_____

2. What clues in the passage let you know this? _____

_____

3. Has Connie been doing well so far? How do you know? _____

_____

She feels her skates leave the ice. She spins through the air and lands with a glide. The crowd goes wild! After Connie leaves the ice, she looks up at the scoreboard and smiles. Her coach runs to hug her.

4. What has Connie just accomplished? _____

5. How do you know this? _____

_____

6. Why does she smile? _____

7. Based on what you have read, write the last sentence of the story.

_____

SCHOOL-HOME CONNECTION With your child, play a mime game in which you act out an athletic event. Ask each other to describe the actions.

23

Practice Book
Changing Patterns

Name _____

Skill Reminder • **A compound subject** is two or more subjects that share a predicate. • **A compound predicate** is two or more predicates that share a subject. • **Use** commas to separate three or more subjects or predicates.

▶ Underline each compound subject once and each compound predicate twice. Then write *compound subject* or *compound predicate*.

1. Swimming and softball are two sports in the Olympic Games.

   _____

2. The swimmer's skill and speed made him a winner.

   _____

3. The runner worked hard and succeeded.

   _____

4. She pitched a perfect game and got a gold medal.

   _____

5. Her friends and family cheered for her in the stands.

   _____

▶ Rewrite each sentence, placing commas where they are needed. Underline each compound subject once and each compound predicate twice.

6. Your bat ball and glove are on the bench.

   _____

7. The ballplayer swimmer and runner come from the same town.

   _____

8. The girl can run fast jump far and throw hard.

   _____

Practice Book
Changing Patterns

Skill Reminder Many words have **consonant blends**.
Some common ones are *str* and *st*.

▶ Fold the paper along the dotted line. As each
spelling word is read aloud, write it in the
blank. Then unfold your paper, and check
your work. Practice spelling any words
you missed.

1. _____

2. _____

3. _____

4. _____

5. _____

6. _____

7. _____

8. _____

9. _____

10. _____

11. _____

12. _____

13. _____

14. _____

15. _____

SPELLING WORDS

1. least
2. fast
3. just
4. burst
5. strip
6. stick
7. strike
8. artist
9. almost
10. student
11. strong
12. start
13. blast
14. step
15. street

© Harcourt

25

Practice Book
Changing Patterns

Name _____

▶ **Write the Vocabulary Word that best completes each
sentence in the story.**

trained	wise	message	patiently	litter	eager

One evening I drank orange juice at the beach. Afterward, I threw

the straw on the sand. "It's not good to **(1)** _____,"
said a voice near my foot. I looked down and saw a sea turtle waiting

(2) _____ for me to respond. "I'm sorry," I said, picking

up the straw. "I should not throw my trash on the beach. I'm

(3) _____ to do the right thing from now on."

"Just by setting a good example, you spread the

(4) _____," the turtle said. "All people should be

(5) _____ to throw trash in trash cans." Just then my

little brother appeared. "Who are you talking to?" he asked. "A

(6) _____ turtle," I said. "Down there." But when we

looked the turtle was gone. "Come on," I said to my brother. "I've got
to find a trash can."

**TRY
THIS!** Imagine that a turtle thanked you for throwing a wrapper into a trash
can. Write a short conversation between you and the turtle using at
least two of the Vocabulary Words.

Practice Book
Changing Patterns

Name _____

▶ **Read the paragraph. Circle the letter of the best answer to each question.**

Taking Care of Your Pet Turtle

Turtles make wonderful pets. They are also easy to take care of. Pet turtles do not need bicycles. They will not make you take them to fancy restaurants. Pet turtles do need homes, though.

Pet turtles live in water tanks. You should find a tank that is at least as large as a shoe box. You will need to put a small dish of clean water in the tank for the turtle to swim in. This water is for the turtle only. Don't even put your pinkie toe in there! Sometimes, turtles like to climb out of the water to sunbathe. This means that the tank also needs a rock for the turtle to climb on. Do not worry. You do not need to find tiny bathing suits, because turtles do not wear them.

---

1 What is the author's purpose in the the first sentence?

    A to persuade

    B to entertain

    C to inform

    D to express

> **💡 Tip**
>
> Why did the author write the first sentence?

2 Which sentence did the writer create to <u>entertain</u> us?

    F You should find a tank that is as least as large as a shoe box.

    G Pet turtles live in water tanks.

    H Sometimes, turtles like to climb out of the water to sunbathe.

    J Pet turtles do not need bicycles.

3 Which sentence was written to <u>inform</u> us?

    A You do not need to find tiny bathing suits.

    B They will not make you take them to fancy restaurants.

    C Pet turtles live in water tanks.

    D Pet turtles do not need bicycles.

 SCHOOL-HOME CONNECTION With your child, look through some headlines or titles in a magazine or newspaper. Decide whether the articles are written to persuade, entertain, or inform.

Practice Book
Changing Patterns

© Harcourt

Name _____

▶ **Some turtles live in the sea. Some turtles live on the land. Some turtles are pets and live in houses. The words below relate to the different places where turtles live. Read the words. Then write the words in the groups where they belong.**

tank	beach	soil	heat lamp	grass	box
waves	pond	sand	water dish	ocean	

1. _____

2. _____

3. _____

4. _____

1. _____

2. _____

3. _____

4. _____

1. _____

2. _____

3. _____

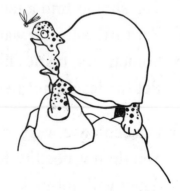

SCHOOL-HOME CONNECTION Put some groceries on the table. Have your child sort the groceries into groups, such as cans, boxes, bags, or cartons. Have your child group the objects in several different ways.

Practice Book
Changing Patterns

© Harcourt

Name _____

Skill Reminder   • **A compound sentence** is two
complete sentences that are joined together.
• **Often, you can use _and_ or _but_ to join the two sentences.**
• **Use a comma (,) before the joining word in a compound sentence.**

▶ **Underline the correct joining word in each compound sentence.**

1. Taro and his sister lived near a bay, **(and/but)** they liked to swim
every day.

2. Taro asked his sister to come with him, **(and/but)** she stayed behind
to collect shells.

3. Jiro-San swept the beach, **(and/but)** Taro helped him.

4. Taro liked Jiro-San, **(and/but)** Yuko did not like him.

5. Taro waited for the turtles, **(and/but)** they did not come.

▶ **Join each pair of sentences with a comma followed by _and_ or _but_.
Write the compound sentences on the lines below.**

6. The whale swam near the boat. Her calf followed her. **(and)**

_____

7. Jiro-San knew many things. He did not know when the turtles would
come. **(but)**

_____

_____

8. It was a warm night. The turtles finally came. **(and)**

_____

9. The baby turtles hatched. They crawled down to the sea. **(and)**

_____

10. Jiro-San is a wise man. Not everyone understands him. **(but)**

_____

Name _____

Skill Reminder   At the beginning of a word, the /n/ sound is sometimes spelled *kn*, and the /r/ sound is sometimes spelled *wr*. The /f/ sound can sometimes be spelled *gh* or *ph*.

▶ Fold the paper along the dotted line. As each spelling word is read aloud, write it in the blank. Then unfold your paper, and check your work. Practice spelling any words you missed.

1. _____

2. _____

3. _____

4. _____

5. _____

6. _____

7. _____

8. _____

9. _____

10. _____

11. _____

12. _____

13. _____

14. _____

15. _____

SPELLING WORDS

1. known
2. written
3. laugh
4. sphere
5. wreck
6. writer
7. wrong
8. wrap
9. wrench
10. knocked
11. knot
12. wring
13. enough
14. rough
15. wrinkle

Practice Book
Changing Patterns

Name _____

▶ **Write the Vocabulary Word that best completes each person's sentence.**

| telegraph | drifts | temperature | guided | trail | splinters |

1. The _____ outside is below freezing.

4. I'm sure your father can stay on the

_____.

2. Maybe we should send a

_____

message to your father.

5. The dogs have

_____

him home before.

3. The _____ of snow are getting higher.

6. Yes, I just hope they don't get any

_____

of ice in their paws.

▶ **Complete the sentence with two Vocabulary Words.**

In one tale, a **(7)** _____ of pebbles

(8) _____ the children home.

TRY THIS! Think about an outdoor experience you have had. Write a paragraph about it using some of the Vocabulary Words.

Practice Book
Changing Patterns

Name _____

▶ **Read the "Things to Do" list. Use the words in dark print to help you fill in the Synonyms and Antonyms charts.**

Things to Do

1. **Buy very warm** gloves for the **cold** weather.
2. **Return** <u>Snow Monster</u> by I. M. **Freezing** to the library.
3. **Take out** book about famous ice skaters.
4. **Try to find** my jacket in the **attic**.
5. **Purchase hot** chocolate at the grocery store.
6. **Look for** my boots in the **basement**.

Synonyms

Synonyms have similar meanings.

1. burning

_____

_____

2. frosty

_____

_____

3. search for

_____

_____

4. pay for

_____

_____

Antonyms

Antonyms have opposite meanings.

5. return

_____

6. hot

_____

7. freezing

_____

8. attic

_____

© Harcourt

Practice Book
Changing Patterns

Name _____

▶ **Read the newspaper clipping. Then circle the letter of the best answer to each question.**

New Medicine Discovered by Lucky Accident

London, October 15, 1928—A new medicine has been discovered by a doctor in England named Alexander Fleming. "This is a very important discovery," Dr. Fleming said. "Now, we will be able to cure many diseases." Dr. Fleming discovered by accident how to make this medicine. He put germs called bacteria in a special container in his laboratory. He also put mold next to the germs. Then Dr. Fleming went on vacation and forgot about his experiment. When he returned from vacation, he discovered something very surprising! The germs had stopped growing, but the mold had kept growing. The mold had killed the germs. Dr. Fleming decided to make a medicine from the mold. He called the medicine penicillin.

1 What is an antonym for *by accident*?

A on purpose

B just because

C for no reason

D luckily

> **Tip**
> Remember that antonyms have opposite meanings.

2 What is a synonym for *special*?

F clean

G pretty

H certain

J important

> **Tip**
> Remember that synonyms have similar meanings.

3 What is an antonym for *forgot*?

A went

B remembered

C decided

D reminded

> **Tip**
> Which answer choice means the opposite of *forgot*?

Practice Book
Changing Patterns

© Harcourt

Name _____

▶ **After you read the message, fill in the chart. Predict what will happen next.**

To: elizabeth@wahoo.com
From: john@wahoo.com
Subject: Flying in a snowstorm?

Dear Elizabeth,

I am supposed to fly to Canada today to visit my grandparents. I am very excited about going. We play hockey and ice-skate when we are there. But I don't know if we will be able to leave! The forecast says that it is going to snow. Sometimes planes won't fly when it snows. I think it takes a lot of snow to close the airport, and it's not snowing yet. It is cloudy, and our flight leaves in two hours. Do you think a snowstorm will make us change our plans?

Your friend,

John

What I Already Know	Clues in the Story	Prediction

SCHOOL-HOME CONNECTION Read a story with your child. Pause after new developments in the story, and ask your child to predict what will happen next.

34

© Harcourt

Name _____

Skill Reminder • **A common noun** names any person, animal, place, or thing. A common noun begins with a lowercase letter.

• **A proper noun** names a particular person, animal, place, or thing. A proper noun begins with a capital letter.

▶ Circle three nouns in each sentence.

1. Tommy bought a sled for Patti.

2. The gift stayed in his house all December.

3. On Monday, snow covered Vermont.

4. The boy slipped on the ice on Tuesday.

5. Little Balto happily pulled the present to the party.

▶ List each noun you circled in the sentences above in the correct column.

Common Nouns	Proper Nouns
_____	_____
_____	_____
_____	_____
_____	_____
_____	_____
_____	_____

Practice Book
Changing Patterns

Skill Reminder You can spell the /ch/ sound with a *ch* or *tch*. The /sh/ sound can be spelled *sh*.

▶ Fold the paper along the dotted line. As each spelling word is read aloud, write it in the blank. Then unfold your paper, and check your work. Practice spelling any words you missed.

1. _____

2. _____

3. _____

4. _____

5. _____

6. _____

7. _____

8. _____

9. _____

10. _____

11. _____

12. _____

13. _____

14. _____

15. _____

SPELLING WORDS

1. shot
2. chance
3. match
4. watch
5. showed
6. shock
7. pushed
8. such
9. crash
10. chew
11. batch
12. hitched
13. sharp
14. mush
15. speech

© Harcourt

Practice Book
Changing Patterns

Name _____

▶ **Write the Vocabulary Word that best completes each
sentence.**

| creature | survived | curious |
| marine | delicate | collapsed |

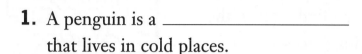

1. A penguin is a _____
   that lives in cold places.

2. _____ animals live
   in or near the sea.

3. Our sand castle _____
   when the wave splashed over it.

4. The elephant seal _____
   the battle.

5. Be careful when you pick up that _____ vase.

6. Cats are very _____ animals;
   they like to look in every box and bag.

▶ **Write the Vocabulary Word with nearly
the same meaning as each word below.**

7. fragile _____

8. animal _____

 TRY THIS! Imagine that you are scuba diving. Write a story about what you see
and do. Use at least three Vocabulary Words.

Practice Book
Changing Patterns

© Harcourt

Name _____

▶ **Read the article. Then circle the letter of the best answer to each question.**

Why Cats Are the Best Pets to Photograph

Cats are the best pets to photograph. Fish, hamsters, and birds are fun, but they are boring subjects for pictures. You can find a cat in the most unusual and interesting places—on a dining room chair, on the living room rug,  on the refrigerator, on the window sill, or under the bed. Cats like to sit in the sunlight, which makes them look pretty. Cats twist their bodies around in all kinds of ways, too. Their tails do funny things, like wag this way and that. Pictures of cats make you smile.

1 What is the author's purpose for writing this article?

  A to entertain

  B to inform

  C to persuade

  D to tell how to do something

 **Tip**
How do you feel about the topic after reading the article?

2 What does the author want you to believe?

  F Fish are boring pets.

  G Cats are the best pets.

  H Cats are the best pets to photograph.

  J Photographers should only take pictures of animals.

 Tip
Ignore answers that are not supported by the article.

3 What is NOT a reason to photograph cats?

  A They make you smile.

  B They do cute things.

  C They look pretty.

  D They are good at catching mice.

 Tip
Be sure to select what is NOT a reason.

SCHOOL-HOME CONNECTION Look at a short passage in a book or magazine with your child. Discuss the author's purpose for writing the passage.

38

Practice Book
Changing Patterns

© Harcourt

Name _____

**Wild Shots,
They're My Life**

Grammar:
Singular and
Plural Nouns

Skill Reminder • A **singular noun** names one person, animal, place, or thing.

• A **plural noun** names more than one person, animal, place, or thing.

▶ Circle the nouns. Write *S* above each singular noun. Write *P* above each plural noun.

1. The photographer takes pictures of animals.

2. Many strange creatures live on those islands.

3. A cactus makes a tasty treat for a tortoise.

4. The iguanas are fighting over some branches.

5. The seal flaps its flippers on the shore.

▶ Write the correct plural form of each singular noun.

6. crab _____

7. monkey _____

8. daisy _____

9. bus _____

10. puppy _____

11. parrot _____

12. canary _____

13. bush _____

14. pouch _____

15. donkey _____

TRY THIS! Make a list of ten singular nouns naming things you see in your classroom. Then write the plural form of each noun.

Practice Book
Changing Patterns

Name _____

▶ **Read the newspaper story. Then circle the letter of the best answer to each question.**

Arizona Herald

T. Rex Alive and Well!

August 12, 2003, Phoenix, Arizona—A <u>live</u> Tyrannosaurus rex was found in a <u>desert</u> in Arizona yesterday. The Tyrannosaurus Rex is one of the largest <u>land</u> animals that ever existed. The boy who discovered the dinosaur reported, "T. Rex was very hungry."

1 Which sentence uses the underlined multiple-meaning word in the same way as the newspaper story?

　A The boy prefers vacationing on the <u>land</u> to vacationing on the sea.

　B I hope the flying dinosaur will <u>land</u> safely.

> 💡 **Tip**
> Which answer means "the ground?"

2 Which sentence uses the underlined homograph in the same way as the newspaper story?

　F Dinosaurs cannot <u>live</u> without water.

　G The hunter brought back a <u>live</u> dinosaur.

> 💡 **Tip**
> Which answer means "to be alive?"

3 Which sentence uses the homograph in the same way as the newspaper story?

　A I was ready to <u>desert</u> the house when I saw the dinosaur peek in.

　B We camped in the <u>desert</u> for two weeks.

> 💡 **Tip**
> Which answer means "a hot, sandy area of land?"

© Harcourt

SCHOOL-HOME CONNECTION With your child, make a short list of words that have more than one meaning. Play a game of charades, acting out the meanings of each word. Have your child guess the words.

42

Practice Book
Changing Patterns

Name _____

Skill Reminder Some **irregular nouns** change their spelling in the plural form.

▶ **Underline the irregular noun in each sentence. Write *S* if the noun is singular. Write *P* if the noun is plural.**

1. Have you ever seen a goose in the

   barn? _____

2. Many mice live in that cave. _____

3. The teeth of some animals are sharp. _____

4. That moose is too big to live in

   your bedroom. _____

5. The men ran away from the volcano. _____

▶ **Write the correct plural form of each singular noun. Use a dictionary if necessary.**

6. woman _____   11. goose _____

7. deer _____   12. child _____

8. sheep _____   13. foot _____

9. trout _____   14. tooth _____

10. man _____   15. mouse _____

 TRY THIS! Pick one singular noun and one plural noun from your list above. Use both words in one sentence.

Practice Book
Changing Patterns

© Harcourt

Name _____

Skill Reminder   You can spell the /oi/ sound *oi* or *oy*.

▶ Fold the paper along the dotted line. As each spelling word is read aloud, write it in the blank. Then unfold your paper, and check your work. Practice spelling any words you missed.

1. _____

2. _____

3. _____

4. _____

5. _____

6. _____

7. _____

8. _____

9. _____

10. _____

11. _____

12. _____

13. _____

14. _____

15. _____

SPELLING WORDS

1. joyful
2. choice
3. voice
4. joint
5. moist
6. spoil
7. royal
8. annoy
9. noise
10. employ
11. soil
12. loyal
13. boiled
14. destroy
15. pointy

© Harcourt

Practice Book
Changing Patterns

Name _____

▶ **Write the Vocabulary Word that best completes each sentence.**

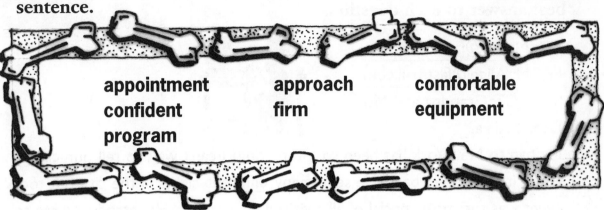

appointment   approach   comfortable
confident   firm   equipment
program

Today, a group of visiting dogs came to our school. The dogs were very

friendly, so I was **(1)** _____ with them. The first

dog to **(2)** _____ me and lick my face was Rosie.

The only pieces of **(3)** _____ she needed were a

harness and a leash. I tried to be very gentle with her. The trainer

said it was also important to be **(4)** _____ so Rosie

could understand my commands. We had a great time together. I would

recommend the visiting dog **(5)** _____ to anyone

who feels lonely and loves animals.

▶ **Complete each sentence with a Vocabulary Word.**

6. If you agree to meet people at a certain time you are

making an _____ with them.

7. If you really believe in yourself, you are very

_____ .

TRY THIS! Write three sentences about somebody who could be helped by a visiting dog. Use at least one of the Vocabulary Words.

Name _____

▶ **Read the e-mail letter. Then circle the letter of the best answer to each question.**

TO: Malika@fastmail.com
FROM: Alice@fastmail.com
SUBJECT: Grandpa and Mo
Dear Malika,

My trip to New York has been so <u>interesting</u>! I can't wait to tell our <u>classmates</u> about it when I get back. I've seen many **different** sights in the city. But today's event was the most special of all. I visited my grandpa. He introduced me to his friend Mo. Mo is not a person. She is a "visiting dog" who has a very <u>important</u> job. She cheers people up who might be sad, sick, or lonely. Mo visits my grandpa one day every week, and he seems very happy about it. I can see why. She is a very friendly dog. I was not at all <u>fearful</u> about meeting her.
See you soon.
Alice

1 What familiar word do you see in the word *interesting*?

   A *inter*
   B *interest*
   C *esting*
   D *ing*

> 💡 **Tip**
> Cover word parts at the beginning or ending with your finger.

2 What two words make up the word *classmates*?

   F *class* and *ate*
   G *room* and *mates*
   H *class* and *mates*
   J *class* and *room*

> 💡 **Tip**
> Look for familiar smaller words inside the word *classmates*.

3 Which correctly separates the word *different* into shorter parts, called syllables?

   A *diff-ere-nt*
   B *di-ff-er-ent*
   C *differ-ent*
   D *dif-fer-ent*

> 💡 **Tip**
> When two or more consonants appear in the middle of a word, divide between them.

SCHOOL-HOME CONNECTION With your child, read a passage from a favorite story. Help your child identify long words and divide them into syllables.

Practice Book
Changing Patterns

© Harcourt

Name _____

Skill Reminder • **A possessive noun** tells who or what something belongs to.

• **A singular possessive noun** shows ownership by one person or thing. Add an apostrophe (') and an *s* to a singular noun to show ownership.

▶ **Circle the possessive noun in each sentence.**

1. A visiting dog's job is to make people happy.

2. Many dogs went to the trainer's class.

3. Rosie lay near the girl's bed.

4. The dog tried to eat the boy's food.

5. Bill's room was very quiet.

▶ **Rewrite each phrase using singular possessive nouns.**

6. the tail of the dog _____

7. the pet that belongs to the girl _____

8. the class of the teacher _____

9. the chair owned by the woman _____

10. the food of the man _____

 TRY THIS! Think of a pet that you, a friend, or a relative owns. Write three sentences about that pet. Use a different singular possessive noun in each sentence.

Practice Book
Changing Patterns

Skill Reminder   The /ou/ sound can be spelled *ow* or *ou*.

▶ Fold the paper along the dotted line. As each
spelling word is read aloud, write it in the
blank. Then unfold your paper, and check
your work. Practice spelling any words
you missed.

1. _____

2. _____

3. _____

4. _____

5. _____

6. _____

7. _____

8. _____

9. _____

10. _____

11. _____

12. _____

13. _____

14. _____

15. _____

SPELLING WORDS

1. crown
2. proud
3. however
4. count
5. crowded
6. around
7. south
8. loud
9. house
10. shouted
11. howl
12. growl
13. bounce
14. fountain
15. sound

© Harcourt

Practice Book
Changing Patterns

Name _____

▶ **Read the Vocabulary Words. Then read the groups of related words in each kite. Write the Vocabulary Word that belongs in each group.**

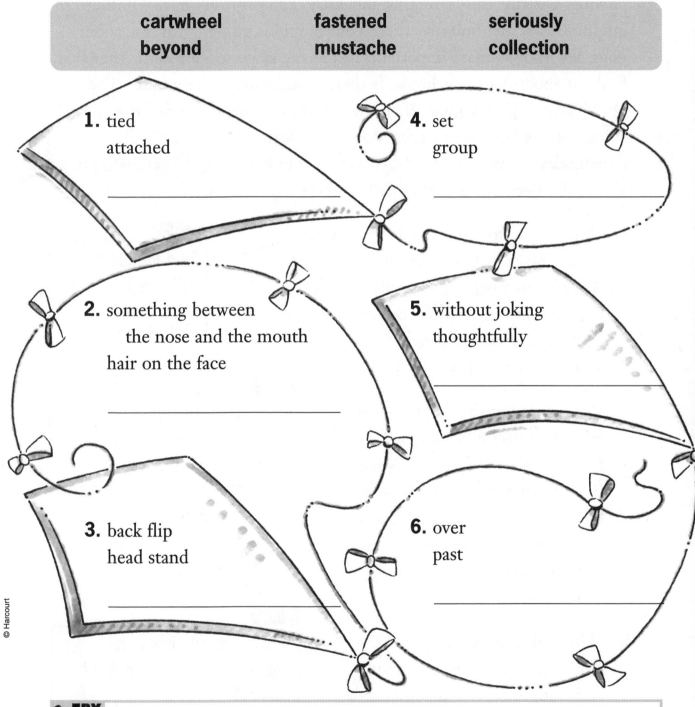

cartwheel	fastened	seriously
beyond	mustache	collection

1. tied
attached

_____

2. something between
the nose and the mouth
hair on the face

_____

3. back flip
head stand

_____

4. set
group

_____

5. without joking
thoughtfully

_____

6. over
past

_____

TRY THIS! Think of one more word to add to each list.

© Harcourt

Practice Book
Changing Patterns

Name _____

▶ **Read the paragraph. Then circle the letter of the best answer to each question.**

Moving begins when you get the news that you and your family are moving. Usually, this is exciting and scary. You probably have a million questions. So, first find out where your family is going. Next, ask about your new room—that's important. Is it as big as your old room? After that, find out about your new home. Is there a backyard? A treehouse? Then you'll have to pack your stuff. You want to make sure your favorite stuffed animal or baseball mitt or dress doesn't get lost by mistake. Finally, when moving day arrives, say good-bye to your old front door. That's what I always do. Because soon after that, you can say hello to your new home.

1 What is the first thing to do when you get the news that your family is moving?

A Find out where your family is going.

B Find out if there is a treehouse.

C Ask a million questions.

D Pack your things.

> **Tip**
> Find the sentence with the sequence word *first*.

2 What question should you ask before you start packing?

F When should I say good-bye?

G Is moving scary and exciting?

H What is interesting and special about my new home?

J Can I take my baseball mitt with me?

> **Tip**
> Find the words *pack your stuff.* Then look at the sentences before those words.

3 Which of these words is NOT a sequence word in the paragraph?

A begins   **C** when

B make sure   **D** finally

> **Tip**
> Which answer choice does not help explain the order of events?

© Harcourt

SCHOOL-HOME CONNECTION Look through the newspaper with your child. Read an article about an event that interests both of you. Then ask your child to retell the story in chronological order, using sequence words such as *first, next, then, yesterday, next year,* and *a week ago.*

50

Practice Book
Changing Patterns

Name _____

▶ **Read the newspaper story. Then circle the letter of the best answer to each question.**

March 1—Cambridge Elementary School. Yesterday, Chelsea Martinez lost her sparkling magic marker. She remembered that she had the magic marker before lunch. "Then after recess I looked for it in my backpack, and it was gone," she said. This morning, everyone searched the classroom, the lunchroom, and the hall. "So far," Karen Ho said, "it hasn't turned up. And I should know because Chelsea is my best friend." Karen told us that the sparkling marker was very special to Chelsea. "I gave it to her a week ago for her birthday." If anyone finds a sparkling magic marker, please give it back to Chelsea. "Next year, when I get such a great present for my birthday, I am definitely going to keep it at home," Chelsea said.

1 When is Chelsea's birthday?
  A at the end of February
  B January 3, 1991
  C March 1
  D in December

💡 **Tip**
Find the sequence words *a week ago.*

2 How do you know?
  F She could not find her marker.
  G Karen Ho gave her the sparkling marker, and she is Chelsea's best friend.
  H The newspaper article is dated March 1, and Chelsea's birthday was the week before.
  J Next year, Chelsea will keep her birthday presents at home.

💡 **Tip**
Find the date of the article.

3 Which sequence word tells you when Chelsea lost her marker?
  A Last week
  B Yesterday
  C This morning
  D Next year

💡 **Tip**
Think about when the whole series of events began.

Practice Book
Changing Patterns

© Harcourt

Name _____

► **Read the directions for making a Wish Kite. Then answer the questions below.**

Make a Wish Kite

Materials	Directions
2 sticks	**1.** Cut the newspaper into a diamond shape.
newspaper	**2.** Cross two sticks, and tie them to the newspaper kite.
rags	**3.** Write wishes on pieces of paper.
paper	**4.** Knot the wishes into rags to make the kite's tail.
paste	**5.** Tie string to the kite, and fly it.
pencil	**6.** For the Wish Kite to work, there should be no
string	wishes in the tail when the kite is taken down.

1. What is the <u>first</u> thing you need to do to make the Wish Kite—cross

two sticks or cut newspaper? _____

2. What is the <u>next</u> thing you need to do—cross two sticks or make

kite tail? _____

3. <u>Then</u>, what do you need to do—knot wishes into rags or write

wishes? _____

4. <u>Finally</u>, what do you need to do—fly kite or make tail with wishes?

_____

► **What has to happen for the Wish Kite to work?**

_____

_____

► **Write a wish that you would tie into a Wish Kite's tail.**

_____

SCHOOL-HOME CONNECTION Talk with your child about a
favorite thing you like to do together, such as baking cookies,
making an art project, or cooking breakfast. Help your child
write down the directions in 3 or 4 simple steps, using
signal words such as *first, next, then,* and *finally.*

© Harcourt

Practice Book
Changing Patterns

Name _____

Skill Reminder • **A plural possessive noun** shows ownership by more than one person or thing.

• To show ownership, add only an apostrophe (') to a plural noun that ends in *s*.

▶ **Write the plural possessive noun in each sentence.**

1. The boys' parents work hard. _____

2. The neighbors' yards are neat. _____

3. Where are the racers' bicycles? _____

4. The bikes' tires are flat. _____

5. Julian pretends to drive his parents' car. _____

▶ **Rewrite each phrase, using a plural possessive noun.**

6. the kites of the girls _____

7. the games of the friends _____

8. the nests of the birds _____

9. the jobs of the adults _____

10. the bones of the puppies _____

 TRY THIS! Write three plural nouns that end with *s*. Then write the plural possessive form of each noun.

Name _____

Skill Reminder   • **A plural possessive noun** shows ownership by more than one person or thing. To show ownership, add only an apostrophe (') to a plural noun that ends in *s*.

▶ Fold the paper along the dotted line. As each spelling word is read aloud, write it in the blank. Then unfold your paper, and check your work. Practice spelling any words you missed.

1. _____

2. _____

3. _____

4. _____

5. _____

6. _____

7. _____

8. _____

9. _____

10. _____

11. _____

12. _____

13. _____

14. _____

15. _____

SPELLING WORDS

1. brother's
2. brothers
3. uncle's
4. uncles
5. sister's
6. sisters
7. sisters'
8. man's
9. men's
10. child's
11. girls
12. girl's
13. girls'
14. mine
15. yours

© Harcourt

Practice Book
Changing Patterns

▶ **Write the Vocabulary Word that best completes each sentence.**

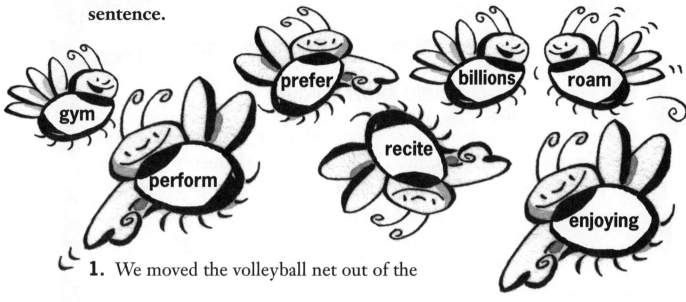

1. We moved the volleyball net out of the

   _____ to make room for our talent show.

2. The audience seems to be _____ the show.

3. My best friend, Amandeep, is going to play a drum solo.

   I can't wait to see her _____!

4. Marco plans to _____ a poem from memory.

5. Emily and Sacha _____ to show a video they made.

6. Keisha will give a speech about the _____ of stars in the sky.

▶ **Write the Vocabulary Word that means the opposite of each word below.**

7. disliking   _____

8. a few   _____

TRY THIS! Write a paragraph about the last talent show you saw. Use as many of the Vocabulary Words as you can.

© Harcourt

Name _____

▶ **Read the advertising poster for a magic show. Then complete the chart below.**

 MAGIC SHOW TONIGHT

Come one, come all, to the most wonderful magic show on Earth! It is a celebration of nonstop magic. The best magic performer in the world will put you under a spell. Watch rabbits disappear and then reappear again. See the best tricks imaginable for yourself!

WHEN: 7:00 P.M.
WHERE: Tuttle Grammar School

	Prefix	What Prefix Means	+ Root Word	= New Word	New Word Means
1.	non-	not-	stop	nonstop	without stopping
2.					
3.					

	Root Word	+ Suffix	What Suffix Means	= New Word	New Word Means
4.					
5.					
6.					
7.					

SCHOOL-HOME CONNECTION With your child, play a guessing game. Say what you want a word to mean when a prefix or suffix is added, and ask your child to guess the new word. For example: Question: "How would you say *able to break*?" Response: "Breakable."

Practice Book
Changing Patterns

© Harcourt

▶ **This newspaper story contains incomplete words that
are underlined. Choose the prefix or the suffix that
belongs with each underlined word. Circle the letter next to your choice.**

MARCH • THE NEWSPAPER • 25¢

The talent show at Grimley Grammar School was **(1)** enjoy. Everyone
had a wonderful time. The students put on a great **(2)** product. Mrs.
Eaton should be **(3)** joyed. One of her students, Beany, was the main
(4) attract of the night. Beany's somersaults and cartwheels were so
amazing that they were almost **(5)** unbeliev. In fact, Mary Esther, who
played a queen bee, was so surprised that she looked on in **(6)** belief.
Erin, Harumi, and Laticia performed a dance, and Barrett's band played
two songs.

1 enjoy
A dis
B non
C over
D able

2 product
F able
G over
H ion
J non

3 joyed
A over
B non
C dis
D able

4 attract
F dis
G over
H non
J ion

5 unbeliev
A dis
B able
C non
D ion

6 belief
F dis
G able
H over
J ion

💡 **Tip**

Does your choice sound right? Does the meaning
of the new word make sense in the story?

Practice Book
Changing Patterns

▶ **Read the paragraph. Then write *valid* or *invalid* next to each conclusion below. Remember to use information from both the story and what you already know to draw conclusions.**

(1) I was so excited when I found out about the school play. Plays are fun to see. **(2)** I thought it would be even more fun to be in one. **(3)** I guessed that I would be the star of the play. **(4)** After all, who knew more about plays than I did? **(5)** It turned out that my teacher, Mr. Li, knew more. **(6)** He even knew that I would not be the star. **(7)** In fact, I had a tiny part in the play! I only said three words, "Yes, your majesty." I felt silly saying my puny little line. **(8)** Maybe that is why Mr. Li said, "Don't worry. Future stars have to start somewhere."

1. The author likes plays. _____

2. The author did not want to be in the play. _____

3. The author was the star of the play. _____

4. Mr. Li knows more than the author about plays. _____

5. Mr. Li knows more than anyone else about plays. _____

6. Mr. Li decided not to give the author a big part. _____

7. The author was unhappy about having a small part. _____

8. Mr. Li believes the author may be a star someday. _____

© Harcourt

Skill Reminder • An **abbreviation** is a short way to write a word. Use a period after most abbreviations.
• Begin abbreviations for proper nouns with capital letters.

▶ **Rewrite these abbreviations correctly.**

1. jan. 15 _____

6. dr. Kerry _____

2. mr. Sands _____

7. tues. _____

3. apr. 17 _____

8. High st. _____

4. wed. _____

9. ms. ruhl _____

5. Grand ave. _____

10. mrs. ford _____

▶ **Rewrite each phrase, using abbreviations correctly.**

11. December 20

16. Mister Yung

_____

_____

12. Lambert Road

17. Central Avenue

_____

_____

13. August 14

18. Doctor Soto

_____

_____

14. Thursday, May 9

19. Sunday, November 3

_____

_____

15. February 12

20. Long Lake Street

_____

_____

TRY THIS! Write out an envelope to send a letter to your teacher. Use abbreviations for your teacher's name and school address.

© Harcourt

Practice Book
Changing Patterns

Skill Reminder The /ô/ sound you hear in *boss, paw,*
and *haul* can be spelled *o, aw,* or *au*.

▶ Fold the paper along the dotted line. As each
spelling word is read aloud, write it in the
blank. Then unfold your paper, and check
your work. Practice spelling any words
you missed.

1. _____

2. _____

3. _____

4. _____

5. _____

6. _____

7. _____

8. _____

9. _____

10. _____

11. _____

12. _____

13. _____

14. _____

15. _____

SPELLING WORDS

1. song
2. law
3. because
4. soft
5. dawn
6. crawl
7. lost
8. taught
9. long
10. pause
11. frost
12. lawn
13. hawk
14. laundry
15. author

© Harcourt

Practice Book
Changing Patterns

Name _____

▶ **Write the Vocabulary Word that best completes each sentence.**

| ballhawk | vanish | fault | concentrate | outfielder | depend |

1. That ball you hit seemed to _____ into the air!

2. That's right! We really _____ on your hitting to win the game!

3. Wasn't it my _____ the other team got that third run?

4. Not at all! No _____ could have caught that ball.

5. I really tried to _____ on my fielding today.

6. Well, you're a real _____. Not much gets by you!

▶ **Solve these equations using Vocabulary Words.**

7. a toy + a bird =

_____

8. not in + meadow + *er* =

_____

9. motor vehicle + *ish* =

_____

 TRY THIS! Make up titles for three books about sports, using a Vocabulary Word in each title.

Practice Book
Changing Patterns

© Harcourt

Name _____

▶ **Read the following history of baseball. Then circle the letter of the best answer to each question.**

The History of Baseball

A game like baseball was first played in England in the 1700s. The English game was called rounders. In rounders, you could put a player out of the game by throwing the ball at him and hitting him when he ran from base to base.

Baseball became a different game from rounders after a New Yorker, Alexander Cartwright, wrote a set of baseball rules in 1845. He decided that you had to put a player out by tagging him with the ball instead. The new rule made baseball into a very different game.

Baseball became a popular American sport when soldiers began to play the game during the Civil War (1861-65). After the war, baseball teams formed all over the country.

1 Which event occurred first in the history of baseball?

　A Soldiers played baseball during the Civil War.

　B A game called rounders was played in England.

　C The game was invented in 1845.

　D Alexander Cartwright wrote rules for baseball.

> 💡 **Tip**
> Look for time-order clues in the dates in the text.

2 Which event occurred next in the history of baseball?

　F Alexander Cartwright wrote rules for baseball.

　G Baseballs became smaller and harder.

　H Soldiers played baseball during the Civil War.

　J Baseball teams formed all over the country.

> 💡 **Tip**
> Put the events in order from first to last.

SCHOOL-HOME CONNECTION With your child, draw a sequence chart of four boxes connected by arrows. Write one major event in baseball history in each box. Invite your child to draw a picture to go with each box.

Practice Book
Changing Patterns

© Harcourt

Name _____

Skill Reminder   • **A singular pronoun** takes the place
of a singular noun. Always capitalize the pronoun *I*.
Singular Pronouns: *I, me, you, he, she, him, her, it*
• **A plural pronoun** takes the place of a plural noun.
Plural Pronouns: *we, us, you, they, them*

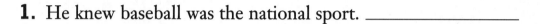

▶ **Write the pronoun in each sentence. Put *S* beside it if it
is a singular pronoun, and *P* if it is a plural pronoun.**

1. He knew baseball was the national sport. _____

2. They talked about last night's game. _____

3. She was very bored at ball games. _____

4. You jumped out of your seat when the team won. _____

5. Charles saw them on the ballfield. _____

▶ **Use a singular or plural pronoun to replace each underlined phrase.**

6. <u>Marco and his uncle</u> ate ice cream after the first inning.

   _____ ate ice cream after the first inning.

7. <u>Roberta</u> hit the ball over the fence.

   _____ hit the ball over the fence.

8. The coach asked <u>Bill and me</u> to go to practice.

   The coach asked _____ to go to practice.

9. Was <u>the field</u> muddy after the rainstorm?

   Was _____ muddy after the rainstorm?

10. Raymond took <u>his sister</u> to the ballpark.

    Raymond took _____ to the ballpark.

Practice Book
Changing Patterns

Skill Reminder   The vowel sound you hear in *zoo* and *soup* can be spelled *oo* or *ou*. The vowel sound you hear in *foot* is usually spelled *oo*.

▶ Fold the paper along the dotted line. As each spelling word is read aloud, write it in the blank. Then unfold your paper, and check your work. Practice spelling any words you missed.

1. _____

2. _____

3. _____

4. _____

5. _____

6. _____

7. _____

8. _____

9. _____

10. _____

11. _____

12. _____

13. _____

14. _____

15. _____

SPELLING WORDS

1. boots
2. grouped
3. shook
4. school
5. looked
6. hood
7. choose
8. brook
9. zoomed
10. balloon
11. loose
12. soot
13. understood
14. cartoon
15. afternoon

Practice Book
Changing Patterns

▶ **Complete the diary entry. Write the Vocabulary Word that best completes each sentence.**

glanced	comfort	longed	contagious
prescription	attention	unexpected	

Dear Diary,

Monday

Today I **(1)** _____ at myself in the mirror.

I saw an **(2)** _____ sight. I had red spots on

my face! I had measles! Measles is a **(3)** _____

sickness. Now I have to stay home. Myra says I am just trying to get

(4) _____. But I really am sick.

Tuesday

Last night I **(5)** _____ to be back at school.

I miss my friends. I feel a little bit better today. It is a

(6) _____ to know that I won't have these

spots forever!

Well, it's time for me to go. My mom says it is time for me to

take my **(7)** _____ medicine.

▶ **Write a sentence using two Vocabulary Words that have three syllables.**

8. _____

_____

_____

Practice Book
Changing Patterns

© Harcourt

Name _____

▶ This nonsense poem is filled with prefixes and suffixes.
Read the poem. Then circle the letter of the best answer
to each questions.

Aunt Ida likes nonfiction.
Aunt Sue dislikes the zoo.
When Aunt Lou makes a prediction,
It's almost always untrue.

Aunt Sheila sometimes oversleeps,
Though Aunt Gloria disapproves.
Aunt Bea disappears into heaps
Of boxes when she moves.

Aunt Rita likes perfection,
So redo what you've done.
Aunt Bea has the best selection
Of readable books. She's fun!

1 What does the poem tell you about
Aunt Lou's predictions?
A They always come true.
B They almost never come true.
C They almost always come true.
D They never come true.

Tip
Think about
what the
prefix *-un*
means.

2 When does Aunt Gloria disapprove of Aunt Sheila?
F when Aunt Sheila doesn't sleep
G when Aunt Sheila goes to sleep
H when Aunt Sheila doesn't get enough sleep
J when Aunt Sheila sleeps too much

Tip
Consider the
meanings of
the prefixes
"dis-" and
"over-".

3 What is the OPPOSITE of a
readable book?
A a book you have already read
B a book you would like to read
C an unreadable book
D a re-readable book

Tip
Think about the meaning
of the suffix *-able*. Then
think about prefixes that
would say "the opposite of
able to."

SCHOOL-HOME CONNECTION With your child, find and
underline all the words in the poem that contain a prefix or a
suffix. Cover up the prefix or the suffix of each word.
Ask your child to read the root word.

Practice Book
Changing Patterns

© Harcourt

Skill Reminder • **A subject pronoun** takes the place of one or more nouns in the subject of a sentence.
Subject Pronouns: *I, you, he, she, it, we, they*
• **Capitalize pronouns when they begin a sentence.**

► **Write the subject pronoun in each sentence.**

1. She was a cute baby. _____

2. It was hard to understand baby talk. _____

3. They made funny faces to make her laugh. _____

4. He threw his bottle and kicked his feet in the air. _____

5. I peeked into the crib to see the baby. _____

► **Use a subject pronoun to replace each underlined phrase.**

6. <u>The two babies</u> rolled around on the floor.

   _____ rolled around on the floor.

7. <u>Bianca</u> sat in her high chair eating a banana.

   _____ sat in her high chair eating a banana.

8. <u>Pablo's father</u> made a tower of blocks for the children.

   _____ made a tower of blocks for the children.

9. <u>The stuffed bunny</u> was Marvin's favorite toy.

   _____ was Marvin's favorite toy.

10. <u>Carla and I</u> baby-sat for the newborn baby.

    _____ baby-sat for the newborn baby.

Practice Book
Changing Patterns

Skill Reminder   The vowel sound you hear in *yard* is usually spelled *ar*.

▶ Fold the paper along the dotted line. As each spelling word is read aloud, write it in the blank. Then unfold your paper, and check your work. Practice spelling any words you missed.

1. _____

2. _____

3. _____

4. _____

5. _____

6. _____

7. _____

8. _____

9. _____

10. _____

11. _____

12. _____

13. _____

14. _____

15. _____

SPELLING WORDS

1. started
2. card
3. park
4. smart
5. star
6. shark
7. mark
8. barber
9. party
10. pardon
11. bark
12. tart
13. carpet
14. farther
15. barn

© Harcourt

Practice Book
Changing Patterns

Name _____

▶ **Write the Vocabulary Word that best completes each sentence.**

generation   persistently   illuminated   summoned   faithful   fortunate

1. If you are a lucky person, you are _____.

2. If something is lit up, it is _____.

3. A group of family members born around the same time form a

   _____.

4. If your mother called you in to dinner,

   she _____ you.

5. A very loyal person is _____.

6. I felt _____ to have such loyal friends.

7. If you keep trying to do something, you are working

   _____.

8. My grandparents belong to a different _____ than I do.

9. The candles _____ the room.

TRY THIS! Write a paragraph about a tradition you share with your family. It can be a holiday tradition, a birthday tradition, or something you and your family like to do together. Use at least two Vocabulary Words.

Practice Book
Changing Patterns

Name _____

HOMEWORK
**Sayings We Share:
Proverbs and
Fables**
Narrative Elements
TEST PREP

▶ **Read the passage. Then circle the letter of the best answer to each question.**

Bear liked to ride his bicycle. It was his favorite thing to do. But he also needed to practice playing his tuba for the school band. "I know," he decided, "I'll practice the tuba while I ride my bike!"

Bear picked up the big tuba, went into the garage, and climbed on his bicycle. It was hard to hold on to the handlebars and play the tuba at the same time. "I'll just pedal," he thought. "I don't need to hold on."

Bear pedaled along the forest path, but the tuba was too heavy. He swayed from side to side just trying to hold it up. He couldn't play it at all. He also couldn't see where he was going. Then—BANG! Bear rode right into a tree. Down went Bear, the bike, and the tuba. Bear remembered a wise saying he read in school: *Don't spread yourself too thin.* "I guess I'll have to practice the tuba before I ride," Bear thought. "I can't do both at once."

1 What is Bear's problem?

   A Bear plays the tuba in the school band.

   B Bear does not know how to ride a bike.

   C Bear likes to ride his bicycle.

   D Bear wants to ride his bike and practice the tuba.

> 💡**Tip**
> Two of the answer choices are not problems.

2 What does Bear learn when he tries to play and ride at the same time?

   F You don't need to hold the handlebars.

   G You shouldn't do too many things at once.

   H Don't lose too much weight.

   J Wise sayings are always true.

> 💡**Tip**
> Eliminate answer choices that are clearly wrong.

3 How will Bear solve his problem?

   A He will practice playing the tuba.

   B He will stop playing and ride his bike instead.

   C He will spread himself too thin.

   D He will ride his bike after practicing the tuba.

> 💡**Tip**
> Look for a quote from Bear about his problem.

SCHOOL-HOME CONNECTION Ask your child to think about a time when he or she has tried to do two things at once. Ask what problems occurred and how your child solved them.

70

© Harcourt

Name _____

Skill Reminder • An **object pronoun** follows an action verb or a word, such as *about, at, for, from, near, of, to,* or *with.*

• Object Pronouns: *me, you, him, her, it, us, them*

• Use *I* and *me* last with other nouns and pronouns.

▶ **Underline the object pronoun in each sentence.**

1. The hare learned a great lesson from him.
2. The wolf ran away from them.
3. They learned proverbs from us.
4. She gave the books to me.
5. I want to read these fables with you.

▶ **Rewrite each sentence. Use an object pronoun to replace the underlined words.**

6. The rooster woke <u>the other farm animals</u>.

_____

7. You could learn a lot from <u>our teacher, Miss Pilmar</u>.

_____

8. I gave <u>Jack, the dog</u>, his delicious dinner.

_____

9. He took <u>the book of fables</u>.

_____

10. The lazy mouse tried to take some cheese from <u>my friend and me</u>.

_____

© Harcourt

Practice Book
Changing Patterns

Name _____

Skill Reminder   The vowel sound you hear in *bear, fair,* and *care* can be spelled *air, ear,* or *are.*

▶ Fold the paper along the dotted line. As each spelling word is read aloud, write it in the blank. Then unfold your paper, and check your work. Practice spelling any words you missed.

1. _____

2. _____

3. _____

4. _____

5. _____

6. _____

7. _____

8. _____

9. _____

10. _____

11. _____

12. _____

13. _____

14. _____

15. _____

SPELLING WORDS

1. bear
2. tear
3. haircut
4. stairs
5. wear
6. airplane
7. compare
8. repair
9. pear
10. prepare
11. stare
12. glare
13. sharing
14. fairy
15. aware

© Harcourt

Practice Book
Changing Patterns

Skills and Strategies Index

COMPREHENSION

GRAMMAR

LITERARY RESPONSE AND ANALYSIS

SPELLING

RESEARCH AND INFORMATION

VOCABULARY

· TROPHIES ·

End-of-Selection Tests

Grade 3-1

Officer Buckle and Gloria

Grade 3-1

Directions: For items 1–18, fill in the circle in front of the correct answer. For items 19–20, write the answer.

Vocabulary

1. We will be careful so we won't have an _____ .
Ⓐ obeys   Ⓑ accident
Ⓒ express   Ⓓ fall

2. The _____ listened when Officer Buckle gave his safety speech.
Ⓐ audience   Ⓑ obeys
Ⓒ expression Ⓓ announce

3. Officer Buckle _____ Gloria to sit during the speech.
Ⓐ noticed   Ⓑ department
Ⓒ commands   Ⓓ announces

4. Mom buys milk in the dairy _____ of the grocery store.
Ⓐ audience   Ⓑ department
Ⓒ noticed   Ⓓ accident

5. I can tell you are happy by the _____ on your face.
Ⓐ expression Ⓑ audience
Ⓒ commands   Ⓓ obeys

6. When Mike follows directions, he _____ the teacher.
Ⓐ commands   Ⓑ noticed
Ⓒ accident   Ⓓ obeys

Practice Book
Changing Patterns

7. By the pond, we _____ a small green frog.
Ⓐ audience   Ⓑ noticed
Ⓒ commands   Ⓓ department

Comprehension

8. In the beginning of the book, why is there snoring during Officer Buckle's speech?
Ⓐ The students are tired.   Ⓑ It is late at night.
Ⓒ The room is dark.   Ⓓ The speech is boring.

9. While Officer Buckle is speaking, Gloria _____ .
Ⓐ barks loudly   Ⓑ sleeps
Ⓒ acts out what he is saying   Ⓓ does tricks he has taught her

10. Officer Buckle thinks the children are cheering for him because he is _____ .
Ⓐ giving them important safety tips
Ⓑ speaking with expression
Ⓒ telling funny jokes
Ⓓ smiling a lot

11. How are the thank-you letters from Napville School alike?
Ⓐ All the students print their letters.
Ⓑ All the letters have drawings of Gloria.
Ⓒ None of them say anything about Gloria.
Ⓓ They have pictures of Officer Buckle and Gloria.

12. Officer Buckle's phones start ringing because _____ .

  Ⓐ the phones aren't working right

  Ⓑ there is a lot of crime

  Ⓒ people want to hear Officer Buckle

  Ⓓ people want to see Gloria

13. When Officer Buckle watches the news, he learns
that _____ .

  Ⓐ he looks good on television

  Ⓑ Gloria is making people laugh

  Ⓒ his speeches are too long

  Ⓓ he does not speak loudly enough

14. How does Officer Buckle feel after he sees himself on TV?

  Ⓐ tired   Ⓑ foolish

  Ⓒ satisfied   Ⓓ pleased

15. Why does Officer Buckle start giving safety tips again?

  Ⓐ Officer Buckle knows that he and Gloria give the best tips
as a team.

  Ⓑ The principal at Napville School invites him to give a
speech.

  Ⓒ He has nothing else to do.

  Ⓓ He wants to be on television again.

16. When does Officer Buckle begin giving speeches again?

  Ⓐ before there are any accidents at Napville School

  Ⓑ before he treats Gloria to ice cream

  Ⓒ on the day that Gloria falls asleep on the stage

  Ⓓ after Napville School has its biggest accident

Grade 3-1

Practice Book
Changing Patterns

17. Which sentence best tells what the story is about?

   Ⓐ Dogs can be funny.

   Ⓑ A police officer should always work alone.

   Ⓒ Sometimes working with a buddy is best.

   Ⓓ Children should learn 101 safety tips.

18. This book is most like _____.

   Ⓐ realistic fiction   Ⓑ historical fiction

   Ⓒ science fiction   Ⓓ fantasy

19. Name two ways that Claire's thank-you letter is different from the others.

_____

_____

_____

_____

_____

20. Claire sends a letter to Officer Buckle about the accident. As a result, what does he learn about Gloria and himself?

_____

_____

_____

_____

Pepita Talks Twice

Directions: For items 1–18, fill in the circle in front of the correct answer. For items 19–20, write the answer.

Vocabulary

1. My brother said, with a _____, that he didn't like the TV show we were watching.
Ⓐ mumbled   Ⓑ grumble
Ⓒ stubborn   Ⓓ languages

2. Spanish and English are two _____ my brother knows.
Ⓐ exploded   Ⓑ mumbled
Ⓒ languages   Ⓓ stubborn

3. The children _____ into laughter when they watched the funny part in the movie.
Ⓐ exploded   Ⓑ darted
Ⓒ mumbled   Ⓓ streak

4. My sister _____ something under her breath that I couldn't hear.
Ⓐ darted   Ⓑ exploded
Ⓒ stubborn   Ⓓ mumbled

5. The dog ran by us so fast that it looked like a _____ of lightning.
Ⓐ streak   Ⓑ grumble
Ⓒ darted   Ⓓ mumbled

6. When I refuse to eat spinach, Dad says I'm being _____ .
Ⓐ mumbled   Ⓑ stubborn
Ⓒ exploded   Ⓓ streak

Grade 3-1

Practice Book
Changing Patterns

7. The dog _____ out into the street, right into traffic.

Ⓐ stubborn   Ⓑ mumbled

Ⓒ grumble   Ⓓ darted

Comprehension

8. This story most likely takes place in _____ .

Ⓐ modern times

Ⓑ the future

Ⓒ outer space

Ⓓ the past

9. What is the first thing Pepita wants to do after school?

Ⓐ speak both Spanish and English

Ⓑ help Mr. Hobbs at the grocery store

Ⓒ teach her dog, Lobo, a new trick

Ⓓ talk to the deliveryman for Aunt Rosa

10. Pepita is upset because people want her to stop and help them to _____ .

Ⓐ understand others   Ⓑ buy groceries

Ⓒ answer telephone calls   Ⓓ train their dogs

11. When Pepita arrives home from school, what does she find?

Ⓐ Juan has not gone to school that day.

Ⓑ Lobo has followed her into the street.

Ⓒ Juan is teaching Lobo to fetch the ball.

Ⓓ Lobo is asleep in the yard.

12. <u>Lobo</u> is the Spanish word for _____ .
Ⓐ brother
Ⓑ canine
Ⓒ wolf
Ⓓ friend

13. Pepita decides to stop speaking Spanish because she is _____ .
Ⓐ confused at school
Ⓑ tired of helping people
Ⓒ upset with the grocer for asking her to help
Ⓓ teaching the dog a trick

14. What does Pepita mean by "having to speak twice"?
Ⓐ saying things in both Spanish and English
Ⓑ repeating everything she says in English
Ⓒ speaking twice for people to hear her
Ⓓ repeating everything she says in Spanish

15. Why doesn't Lobo come when Pepita calls him Wolf?
Ⓐ Lobo doesn't obey Pepita.
Ⓑ Lobo is tired of playing.
Ⓒ Lobo doesn't know Wolf is his English name.
Ⓓ Lobo is playing fetch with Juan.

16. <u>Abuelita</u> is the Spanish word for _____ .
Ⓐ uncle
Ⓑ dog
Ⓒ father
Ⓓ grandmother

Grade 3-1

Practice Book
Changing Patterns

Grade 3-I

17. Papa tells Pepita that if she doesn't speak Spanish anymore, she will have to _____ .

(A) give up tortillas, enchiladas, and tamales

(B) stop going to school

(C) change her name

(D) miss hearing Grandma's stories

18. What makes Pepita realize that she has acted foolishly?

(A) Lobo won't play with her anymore.

(B) Miguel throws a ball in her yard.

(C) Lobo almost gets hit by a car.

(D) Pepita misses singing Spanish songs.

19. Explain what Pepita does when people ask her for help with Spanish and English.

_____

_____

_____

_____

20. What lesson does Pepita learn by the end of the story?

_____

_____

_____

_____

Practice Book
Changing Patterns

Nate the Great, San Francisco Detective

Directions: For items 1–18, fill in the circle in front of the correct answer. For items 19–20, write the answer.

Vocabulary

1. A person who solves mysteries is a _____ .
(A) detective   (B) positive
(C) case   (D) specific

2. The detective is working on a very important _____ .
(A) specific   (B) positive
(C) case   (D) definitely

3. The teacher gave _____ directions when she prepared the students for the test.
(A) assistant   (B) specific
(C) definitely   (D) case

4. Every good detective needs one _____ to help him.
(A) positive   (B) definitely
(C) returned   (D) assistant

5. We can plan on swimming today because Mom says we'll _____ go to the lake.
(A) specific   (B) definitely
(C) positive   (D) returned

6. Alexis _____ the library book on the date it was due.
(A) returned   (B) case
(C) definitely   (D) positive

Practice Book
Changing Patterns

7. She is _____ she knows the correct answer.
(A) definitely   (B) case
(C) assistant   (D) positive

Comprehension

8. The action in the story begins in an _____ .
(A) exercise   (B) object
(C) automobile   (D) airport

9. Who is Nate supposed to meet at ten o'clock?
(A) Willie   (B) Olivia
(C) Sludge   (D) a chauffeur

10. Nate's cousin can't meet him at the airport because she is _____ .
(A) working on another case
(B) driving the limo
(C) visiting friends
(D) waiting at home for Nate

11. What is the first thing Nate has been asked to find in California?
(A) Booksie's Bookstore   (B) Fang's teeth
(C) Claude's seashell   (D) Olivia's feathered boa

12. Nate offers to take Duncan's case because _____ .
(A) Olivia is too busy
(B) Sludge knows the solution
(C) Willie thinks Nate can help him
(D) Annie calls home

Grade 3-1

© Harcourt

13. The case must be solved by two o'clock because that's when _____ .

Ⓐ the Golden Gate Bridge is closed

Ⓑ Nate must return home

Ⓒ Olivia goes to the police

Ⓓ Duncan is telling his friend the joke

14. After Nate leaves Perry's Pancake House, what does he do?

Ⓐ He goes to the Golden Gate Bridge.

Ⓑ He searches Duncan's freezer.

Ⓒ He goes to Booksie's Bookstore.

Ⓓ He searches Perry's trash.

15. Where does Nate find the book?

Ⓐ on the Golden Gate Bridge

Ⓑ in Duncan's backpack

Ⓒ with the cookbooks

Ⓓ in the back seat of the limo

16. Duncan's book is put in the wrong place because of confusion in the _____ .

Ⓐ cover   Ⓑ price

Ⓒ title   Ⓓ index

17. At the end of the story, what will Nate look for at the Golden Gate Bridge?

Ⓐ Olivia's feathered boa

Ⓑ Claude's seashell

Ⓒ Booksie's bag

Ⓓ Fang's teeth

Practice Book
Changing Patterns

18. The waiter at Perry's Pancake House is angry when Nate asks about Duncan because Duncan _____ .

Ⓐ made a mess there

Ⓑ didn't leave the waiter a tip

Ⓒ ordered mushyberry pancakes

Ⓓ couldn't remember the joke

19. What does Nate mean by the statement "losing hope is the worst thing you can lose"?

_____

_____

_____

_____

_____

. _____

20. How does Nate know where to look for Duncan's book in the bookstore?

_____

_____

_____

_____

_____

Allie's Basketball Dream

Directions: For items 1–18, fill in the circle in front of the correct answer. For items 19–20, write the answer.

Vocabulary

1. Rick _____ for the target.
- Ⓐ pretended
- Ⓑ familiar
- Ⓒ aimed
- Ⓓ monitor

2. The _____ of our team is also one of the best players.
- Ⓐ captain
- Ⓑ pretended
- Ⓒ professional
- Ⓓ familiar

3. The lunchroom _____ says we are very well behaved today.
- Ⓐ familiar
- Ⓑ monitor
- Ⓒ aimed
- Ⓓ professional

4. He _____ to be weak so he wouldn't have to carry the heavy box.
- Ⓐ pretended
- Ⓑ aimed
- Ⓒ monitor
- Ⓓ captain

5. Rose sings well enough to become a _____ singer.
- Ⓐ captain
- Ⓑ pretended
- Ⓒ monitor
- Ⓓ professional

6. Since I had been there before, the road looked _____ .
- Ⓐ familiar
- Ⓑ monitor
- Ⓒ professional
- Ⓓ aimed

Comprehension

7. When my teacher applauded loudly, she _____.
Ⓐ screamed at the students
Ⓑ cornered the principal
Ⓒ clapped her hands
Ⓓ pretended to fall asleep

8. What happens first that starts the events that follow in this selection?
Ⓐ Allie plays basketball at the playground with the boys.
Ⓑ Allie waits for her father to come home from work.
Ⓒ Allie's father brings her a gift.
Ⓓ Allie trades her basketball for a new volleyball.

9. "At the playground, Allie scanned the basketball courts" means she _____ .
Ⓐ looked around the courts   Ⓑ ran around the courts
Ⓒ practiced shooting baskets   Ⓓ jumped rope on the courts

10. How does Allie's dad feel about her playing basketball?
Ⓐ angry   Ⓑ scared
Ⓒ ashamed   Ⓓ proud

11. Allie practices shooting baskets because she wants to _____ .
Ⓐ play basketball with her father
Ⓑ see her friends at the playground
Ⓒ become a good basketball player
Ⓓ play with Domino

© Harcourt

12. Julio refuses to play basketball with Allie because _____ .

Ⓐ she doesn't play well

Ⓑ he doesn't like basketball

Ⓒ he is too proud to play with a girl

Ⓓ he is on his way to play with some other boys

13. Why did Allie decide to become a professional basketball player?

Ⓐ She loved the game she saw at Madison Square Garden.

Ⓑ She listened to her father talk about basketball.

Ⓒ She watched the boys at the playground play basketball.

Ⓓ She got a basketball of her very own.

14. In what sport are the words dribble, slam-dunk, backboard, and rim used?

Ⓐ volleyball   Ⓑ soccer

Ⓒ basketball   Ⓓ baseball

15. Allie tells Buddy about her cousin's trophies because she _____ .

Ⓐ feels like telling a story

Ⓑ wants to prove that girls can play basketball

Ⓒ likes bragging about her cousin

Ⓓ doesn't want to talk about trading her basketball

16. How are Allie and Buddy alike?

Ⓐ Both want to be professional ballplayers.

Ⓑ Both like to play volleyball.

Ⓒ Both are good at jumping rope.

Ⓓ Both play games that others say they shouldn't play.

Practice Book
Changing Patterns

17. When Allie misses a shot, Buddy says, "Don't worry, Allie"
to _____ .
- (A) tease her
- (B) encourage her
- (C) make fun of her
- (D) make her nervous

18. At the end of the story, Allie finally makes a perfect basket
because _____ .
- (A) she keeps on trying
- (B) she is lucky
- (C) she uses a smaller ball
- (D) her father helps her

19. Does Buddy think that his volleyball is worth more or less
than Allie's basketball? Explain.

_____

_____

_____

_____

_____

20. What did Allie like about the game at Madison Square Garden?

_____

_____

_____

_____

_____

The Olympic Games: Where H

Directions: For items 1–18, fi
answer. For items 19–20, wri

Vocabulary

1. In school, my brother is rea
history class.
Ⓐ ancient
Ⓒ stadium

2. My sister and I _____ aga
tennis.
Ⓐ compete   Ⓑ host
Ⓒ earned   Ⓓ medals

3. Dad is the _____ of his office party this year.
Ⓐ earned   Ⓑ record
Ⓒ host   Ⓓ ancient

4. We play our home games at the new _____ .
Ⓐ compete   Ⓑ stadium
Ⓒ ancient   Ⓓ medals

5. The team has won three soccer _____ in the past three years.
Ⓐ medals   Ⓑ compete
Ⓒ ceremonies Ⓓ host

6. I worked hard on the story I wrote, and I _____ a good grade.
Ⓐ host   Ⓑ record
Ⓒ earned   Ⓓ compete

The band gets to play a
Ⓐ stadium
Ⓒ ceremonies

7.

8. The runne
Ⓐ co
Ⓒ

Name _____

Grade 3-1

© Harcourt

Practice Book
Changing Patterns

... all the school _____ .

    Ⓑ medals

    Ⓓ host

... winning the sprint broke an old _____ .

    ...mpete   Ⓑ record

    ...ancient   Ⓓ medals

Comprehension

9. This nonfiction piece is most like a _____ .

    Ⓐ magazine article

    Ⓑ personal narrative

    Ⓒ biography

    Ⓓ fantasy

10. The first Olympic Games took place in _____ .

    Ⓐ France   Ⓑ Greece

    Ⓒ Australia   Ⓓ United States

11. How are the swimming events different today than they were in the first modern games?

    Ⓐ Only men could enter the swimming races.

    Ⓑ Only four swimming strokes are allowed in the races today.

    Ⓒ In the first modern games, swimmers could use only one stroke.

    Ⓓ The Olympics made many swimmers famous.

12. The Olympic Games always begin with a _____ .

    Ⓐ torch carrier   Ⓑ parade of nations

    Ⓒ flag bearer   Ⓓ festival

13. Before the games begin, the athletes _____ .

Ⓐ say the Pledge of Allegiance

Ⓑ take an oath

Ⓒ light the torch

Ⓓ sing the "Star-Spangled Banner"

14. The colored rings in the Olympic flag represent _____ .

Ⓐ a color in every country's flag

Ⓑ the color of the continents

Ⓒ some of the competitions

Ⓓ just the countries in Europe

15. In the ancient Olympics, most of the events were _____ .

Ⓐ swimming and track

Ⓑ track and field

Ⓒ field and swimming

Ⓓ track and diving

16. Track events include all of the following **except** _____ .

Ⓐ javelin

Ⓑ middle-distance running

Ⓒ hurdling

Ⓓ sprints

Practice Book
Changing Patterns

Grade 3-I

17. At Sydney, which swimmer was the winner in the backstroke events?

Ⓐ Lenny Krayzelburg

Ⓑ Mark Spitz

Ⓒ Michael Johnson

Ⓓ Johnny Weissmuller

18. Which sport has just recently been added to the Olympic events?

Ⓐ ice-skating

Ⓑ skateboarding

Ⓒ soccer

Ⓓ ballet

19. What do the athletes promise when they take the Olympic oath?

_____

_____

_____

_____

_____

20. What might be a motto for all Olympic contestants?

_____

_____

_____

Turtle Bay

Directions: For items 1–18, fill in the circle in front of the correct answer. For items 19–20, write the answer.

Vocabulary

1. My dog is _____ to come to me when I call her.
   - Ⓐ patiently
   - Ⓑ trained
   - Ⓒ message
   - Ⓓ litter

2. We learned so much from the old man because he was so _____ .
   - Ⓐ patiently
   - Ⓑ message
   - Ⓒ wise
   - Ⓓ litter

3. I left a _____ with Jack's mom to have him call me when he gets home.
   - Ⓐ message
   - Ⓑ wise
   - Ⓒ trained
   - Ⓓ patiently

4. Ron waited _____ for his friends to arrive.
   - Ⓐ eager
   - Ⓑ trained
   - Ⓒ wise
   - Ⓓ patiently

5. We cleaned up the _____ that people had left on the beach.
   - Ⓐ message
   - Ⓑ litter
   - Ⓒ patiently
   - Ⓓ eager

6. All the students paid attention to the teacher, showing that they were _____ to learn.
   - Ⓐ eager
   - Ⓑ message
   - Ⓒ litter
   - Ⓓ patiently

Practice Book
Changing Patterns

Comprehension

7. This selection most likely takes place in _____ .

(A) the past   (B) the present

(C) the future   (D) fantasyland

8. Jiro-San's secrets are most likely about _____ .

(A) his family   (B) his school

(C) nature   (D) old age

9. Why does Taro like Jiro-San?

(A) He learns things from Jiro-San.

(B) Jiro-San makes him laugh.

(C) Jiro-San lets him sweep the beach.

(D) He likes riding in Jiro-San's boat.

10. In this story, a <u>calf</u> is a _____ .

(A) young turtle   (B) baby whale

(C) small dolphin   (D) little swordfish

11. Jiro-San called the turtles his "old friends" because _____ .

(A) the turtles look old, with wrinkled faces and legs

(B) some of the turtles have been his pets for many years

(C) he has been watching the turtles lay eggs for many years

(D) the turtles are friendly and playful

12. Which of the following best shows that Jiro-San is patient?

(A) He sweeps the beach.

(B) He says that all the fish are his friends.

(C) He waits on the beach for the turtles for four nights.

(D) He rows to a secret cove to look for the turtles.

Practice Book
Changing Patterns

Grade 3-1

13. Where does a turtle put her eggs?

Ⓐ She lays them under rocks.

Ⓑ She digs a hole on a sandy beach for them.

Ⓒ She finds a hole on a beach for them.

Ⓓ She lays them on top of the sand on a beach.

14. Jiro-San sweeps the beach because he wants to _____ .

Ⓐ make holes for the turtles

Ⓑ make it clean and safe for the turtles

Ⓒ collect rocks and shells

Ⓓ make hills of sand

15. When Jiro-San's old friends arrive at the beach, what happens first?

Ⓐ All the turtles lay eggs on the beach.

Ⓑ All the turtles stay in the water until the people leave.

Ⓒ Some of the turtles dig holes.

Ⓓ One turtle makes sure the beach is safe.

16. The author wrote this story to _____ .

Ⓐ tell what Turtle Bay is like

Ⓑ tell what it's like to live by the sea

Ⓒ give information about turtles

Ⓓ explain how to clean up a beach

17. Which word best tells about Taro?

Ⓐ weird　　　　　Ⓑ clever

Ⓒ shy　　　　　　Ⓓ curious

18. According to Jiro-San, one turtle comes to the beach first and lays her eggs because _____ .

Ⓐ she wants to be sure the beach is safe for the others

Ⓑ she swims faster than the other turtles

Ⓒ Jiro-San has not finished picking up the litter

Ⓓ the children are making too much noise

19. The writer wanted to tell what a swimming turtle looks like. What did the author compare a turtle to?

_____

_____

_____

_____

_____

_____

20. How are the turtles like Jiro-San?

_____

_____

_____

_____

_____

Balto, the Dog Who Saved Nome

Directions: For items 1–18, fill in the circle in front of the correct answer. For items 19–20, write the answer.

Vocabulary

1. The train conductor sent a message to the station by _____ .
- Ⓐ temperature
- Ⓑ splinters
- Ⓒ telegraph
- Ⓓ tripped

2. The cowboys _____ the cattle back into the pen.
- Ⓐ drifts
- Ⓑ telegraph
- Ⓒ guided
- Ⓓ survived

3. The _____ of snow beside the road were very high.
- Ⓐ drifts
- Ⓑ guided
- Ⓒ trail
- Ⓓ earned

4. We were glad we had warm coats, because the _____ was dropping fast.
- Ⓐ guided
- Ⓑ temperature
- Ⓒ telegraph
- Ⓓ splinters

5. _____ from wood stuck in my finger.
- Ⓐ Guided
- Ⓑ Drifts
- Ⓒ Splinters
- Ⓓ Trail

6. The dog followed the _____ that would lead it home.
- Ⓐ trail
- Ⓑ guided
- Ⓒ telegraph
- Ⓓ temperature

© Harcourt

Grade 3-I

Comprehension

7. At the beginning of the story, what is the problem in Nome?

Ⓐ Many people are sick with diphtheria.

Ⓑ Nome is 880 miles from Anchorage.

Ⓒ People are dying from the flu.

Ⓓ Telephone lines are frozen.

8. All of the following are reasons why it is difficult to get medicine to Nome **except** _____ .

Ⓐ the sea is frozen, so no ships can sail there

Ⓑ the strong winds prevent planes from flying

Ⓒ trains can't get over the snowdrifts

Ⓓ dog teams can get through the storm

9. How was this trip with the dogs different for Kasson?

Ⓐ It was longer than other trips.

Ⓑ Balto had to guide Kasson and the dogs.

Ⓒ Kasson had never made a trip to Nome.

Ⓓ The trail went across a sea of ice.

10. In this story, <u>mush</u> was _____ .

Ⓐ cold food for the dogs

Ⓑ a command for the dogs to start pulling the sled

Ⓒ a mix of snow and icy water

Ⓓ a hot food that Kasson always ate

11. To what did the writer compare the movement of the sea ice?

Ⓐ a gun being shot

Ⓑ the smoothness of glass

Ⓒ the up and down of a roller coaster

Ⓓ keys on a telegraph

© Harcourt

Practice Book
Changing Patterns

12. The bumpy ice was the worst part of the trail over the sea ice because _____ .

Ⓐ the dogs slipped and skidded

Ⓑ the dogs hurt their paws on the sharp ice

Ⓒ the sled kept turning over

Ⓓ Kasson couldn't see through the falling snow

13. What made the loud cracking sound?

Ⓐ The sea ice split apart.

Ⓑ Someone fired a gun.

Ⓒ A frozen tree branch broke off in the wind.

Ⓓ A runner broke off the sled.

14. How did Balto show that he was smart?

Ⓐ by reaching the town of Safety in fourteen hours

Ⓑ by saving Gunnar Kasson from freezing in the snow

Ⓒ by getting around where the sea ice was breaking up

Ⓓ by getting a team of doctors to the rescue train

15. What made the trip miles longer than Kasson expected?

Ⓐ The airport was closed.

Ⓑ The team missed the town of Safety.

Ⓒ Balto could not find the trail.

Ⓓ The team had to go around the deepest snow.

16. Balto was a good lead dog because he was _____ .

Ⓐ big and fast   Ⓑ friendly and sure-footed

Ⓒ tame and strong   Ⓓ calm and determined

17. Why did Kasson shake his head when people thanked him?

Ⓐ He wanted them to thank Balto, not him.

Ⓑ He wanted to take care of Balto's paws.

Ⓒ He was shaking snow off his head.

Ⓓ He was shivering from the cold.

18. There is a statue of Balto in New York City because

he _____ .

Ⓐ was born in New York   Ⓑ trusted people

Ⓒ was a handsome dog   Ⓓ had great courage

19. Why was a dogsled the only way to get the medicine to Nome?

_____

_____

_____

_____

_____

20. How was Balto different from other dogs that are half Eskimo dog and half wolf?

_____

_____

_____

_____

_____

_____

Wild Shots, They're My Life

Directions: For items 1–18, fill in the circle in front of the correct answer. For items 19–20, write the answer.

Vocabulary

1. The little _____ swimming in the fish tank was fun to watch.
Ⓐ curious   Ⓑ delicate
Ⓒ collapsed   Ⓓ creature

2. I was _____ about all the different sea creatures on the island.
Ⓐ marine   Ⓑ curious
Ⓒ survived   Ⓓ collapsed

3. Be careful with the glass vase because it is very _____ .
Ⓐ delicate   Ⓑ survived
Ⓒ curious   Ⓓ creature

4. Beautiful _____ plants grow beside the ocean.
Ⓐ creature   Ⓑ marine
Ⓒ collapsed   Ⓓ litter

5. Lester _____ into bed after a long day of work.
Ⓐ survived   Ⓑ creature
Ⓒ collapsed   Ⓓ delicate

6. Greta _____ the airplane crash with no injuries.
Ⓐ curious   Ⓑ survived
Ⓒ collapsed   Ⓓ delicate

Practice Book
Changing Patterns

Comprehension

7. This informational selection is most like a _____ .

Ⓐ magazine article Ⓑ textbook

Ⓒ fairy tale Ⓓ biography

8. The author of this selection grew up in _____ .

Ⓐ the United States Ⓑ Antarctica

Ⓒ Europe Ⓓ the Galapagos Islands

9. As an adult, the author is able to take good photos of animals because she _____ .

Ⓐ waits until the animals are used to having her around

Ⓑ travels all over the world

Ⓒ gives food to the animals

Ⓓ has a good camera to take photos

10. The author hurried to take a photo of the penguins because the _____ .

Ⓐ chick was furry

Ⓑ chick was sleeping

Ⓒ parents were walking away

Ⓓ parents were feeding the chick

11. How is a Galapagos Marine Iguana different from other lizards?

Ⓐ It looks like a dragon.

Ⓑ It has sharp claws.

Ⓒ It eats in the ocean.

Ⓓ It has spines on its back.

12. The author was able to take a photo of the iguana because she _____ .

Ⓐ kept her camera out of the water

Ⓑ put her camera in a waterproof case

Ⓒ had a waterproof camera

Ⓓ covered her camera with a mask

13. In Tui De Roy's opinion, what makes a photo exciting?

Ⓐ that the animals are furry and feathered

Ⓑ that the photos are taken on islands

Ⓒ that the animals are rare

Ⓓ that the animals are minding their own business

14. Why were the elephant bull seals fighting?

Ⓐ They were fighting over food.

Ⓑ Fighting was their way of playing.

Ⓒ Each of them wanted to be in charge of the beach.

Ⓓ One was mad because the other one fell on him.

15. According to De Roy, what was it like to take the photo of the elephant seals?

Ⓐ easy   Ⓑ dangerous

Ⓒ funny   Ⓓ boring

16. In this article, <u>shots</u> means _____ .

Ⓐ photographs   Ⓑ guns

Ⓒ needles   Ⓓ cameras

17. Which word best tells how the author feels about wild animals?

Ⓐ annoyed   Ⓑ surprised

Ⓒ scared   Ⓓ curious

18. All the animals in this selection belong to a group of animals that _____ .

   Ⓐ can swim   Ⓑ have scales

   Ⓒ have four legs   Ⓓ live near the ocean

19. When did De Roy start taking photos of animals?

_____

_____

_____

_____

_____

20. List three kinds of birds that the author took photos of.

_____

_____

_____

_____

_____

_____

_____

Little Grunt and the Big Egg

Grade 3-1

Directions: For items 1–18, fill in the circle in front of the correct answer. For items 19–20, write the answer.

Vocabulary

1. When the baby stopped crying, our house became nice and _____ .
Ⓐ escape   Ⓑ peaceful
Ⓒ erupting   Ⓓ lava

2. Our neighbors asked us to eat _____ with them.
Ⓐ brunch   Ⓑ escape
Ⓒ lava   Ⓓ peaceful

3. We used four eggs to make an _____ .
Ⓐ escape   Ⓑ erupting
Ⓒ omelet   Ⓓ earned

4. Because the volcano was _____, people had to leave their homes.
Ⓐ erupting   Ⓑ escape
Ⓒ peaceful   Ⓓ aimed

5. The hot _____ gushed out from the volcano.
Ⓐ brunch   Ⓑ omelet
Ⓒ escape   Ⓓ lava

6. The firefighter tried to _____ from the burning rooftop.
Ⓐ erupting   Ⓑ brunch
Ⓒ escape   Ⓓ peaceful

Comprehension

7. This story is most like a _____ .

Ⓐ nursery rhyme   Ⓑ folktale

Ⓒ mystery   Ⓓ riddle

8. How does Little Grunt get the huge egg home?

Ⓐ carries it on his back

Ⓑ rolls it down a hill

Ⓒ gets his family to help him carry it

Ⓓ makes a mat on which to drag it

9. When the big egg arrives at the cave, everyone is _____ .

Ⓐ angry   Ⓑ nervous

Ⓒ excited   Ⓓ disappointed

10. Mama Grunt decides the egg is so big that she will _____ .

Ⓐ make two omelets

Ⓑ ask more friends to brunch

Ⓒ hatch the egg

Ⓓ be allergic to that kind of egg

11. How does a baby dinosaur end up in the Grunts' cave?

Ⓐ It walks into the cave.

Ⓑ It hatches from the egg.

Ⓒ Chief Rockhead Grunt captures it.

Ⓓ The Ugga-Wugga Tribe brings it.

12. Having George as a pet is a problem because George _____ .

Ⓐ sneezes all the time   Ⓑ bites people

Ⓒ makes loud noises   Ⓓ gets too big

Practice Book
Changing Patterns

13. Little Grunt shows that he misses George by _____ .

   Ⓐ looking for him in the swamp

   Ⓑ meeting him secretly

   Ⓒ drawing pictures of him

   Ⓓ talking about him all the time

14. What makes the cave shake?

   Ⓐ a volcano   Ⓑ an earthquake

   Ⓒ George   Ⓓ a storm

15. Granny Grunt thinks Little Grunt should keep the baby dinosaur because _____ .

   Ⓐ Mama Grunt is serving pancakes for Sunday brunch

   Ⓑ it will make a great ride

   Ⓒ every boy needs to have a pet of his own

   Ⓓ the baby dinosaur is cute

16. Chief Rockhead gives up his job as leader because _____ .

   Ⓐ Papa Grunt asks him to resign

   Ⓑ it is someone else's turn to be leader

   Ⓒ he is tired of being the leader

   Ⓓ he doesn't know how to help everyone escape

17. The author wanted to show that George saves the Grunts quickly. To what did he compare George's speed?

   Ⓐ to the lava pouring down the volcano

   Ⓑ to how long George's neck is

   Ⓒ to saying *Tyrannosaurus rex*

   Ⓓ to how high the steam comes out of the volcano

Grade 3-1

Practice Book
Changing Patterns

18. What does the Grunt family learn by the end of the story?

    Ⓐ Animals are stronger than people.

    Ⓑ People are smarter than animals.

    Ⓒ People and animals can help one another.

    Ⓓ Animals need people to take care of them.

19. Is this story about real or imaginary people and things? Explain how you know.

_____

_____

_____

_____

_____

_____

20. Why is the dinosaur's name changed to Georgina?

_____

_____

_____

_____

_____

Rosie, a Visiting Dog's Story

Directions: For items 1–18, fill in the circle in front of the correct answer. For items 19–20, write the answer.

Vocabulary

1. "Don't touch that!" Dad said to the man in a _____ voice.
   - Ⓐ program
   - Ⓑ firm
   - Ⓒ message
   - Ⓓ comfortable

2. You should always _____ a stray dog with caution.
   - Ⓐ approach
   - Ⓑ equipment
   - Ⓒ appointment
   - Ⓓ confident

3. My soft bed is the most _____ one in the house.
   - Ⓐ comfortable
   - Ⓑ approach
   - Ⓒ equipment
   - Ⓓ program

4. I'm _____ I will do well on the test.
   - Ⓐ approach
   - Ⓑ program
   - Ⓒ appointment
   - Ⓓ confident

5. The science lab in our school has some new _____ this year.
   - Ⓐ comfortable
   - Ⓑ firm
   - Ⓒ equipment
   - Ⓓ confident

6. We watched a television _____ about whales last night.
   - Ⓐ firm
   - Ⓑ equipment
   - Ⓒ approach
   - Ⓓ program

7. Dad picked me up early from school for my doctor's _____ .
   - Ⓐ confident
   - Ⓑ firm
   - Ⓒ comfortable
   - Ⓓ appointment

Grade 3-1

Comprehension

8. One way Rosie is different from most other dogs is that
she _____ .
  Ⓐ loves to play fetch   Ⓑ is a working dog
  Ⓒ likes everybody   Ⓓ is trained to obey

9. A "visiting dog" is a dog _____ .
  Ⓐ whose job is to cheer up people
  Ⓑ whose job is to visit schools
  Ⓒ who is always friendly and gentle
  Ⓓ who visits people in the neighborhood

10. As a puppy, Rosie would not have been a good "visiting dog"
because she was _____ .
  Ⓐ too young   Ⓑ not gentle
  Ⓒ too wild and silly   Ⓓ not trained

11. Rosie first learns how to become a "visiting dog" at _____ .
  Ⓐ puppy kindergarten
  Ⓑ home with her owner
  Ⓒ the homes she visits
  Ⓓ the children's hospital

12. In the selection, "Rosie always had good sense" means that
she _____ .
  Ⓐ was a smart dog
  Ⓑ understood all kinds of people
  Ⓒ learned all her lessons fast
  Ⓓ could make her own decisions

© Harcourt

13. According to the selection, what two things do "visiting dogs" have in common?

Ⓐ They are friendly and like to work.

Ⓑ They are mixed breeds.

Ⓒ They are smart and obedient.

Ⓓ They love people and like to play.

14. The author prepares Rosie for her work by _____ .

Ⓐ being very strict and firm with her

Ⓑ playing games with her and letting her play with other dogs

Ⓒ teaching her to be friendly and to jump on people

Ⓓ letting children pull Rosie's long hair

15. Rosie is taught many different commands so that she _____ .

Ⓐ learns to behave well around different people

Ⓑ can prove that she is smart enough for the job

Ⓒ can prove that she is an obedient dog

Ⓓ must learn to understand different languages

16. Rosie will approach a person only after she is told _____ .

Ⓐ "Don't touch"   Ⓑ "Okay, take it"

Ⓒ "Go say hello"   Ⓓ "Catch-me-if-you-can"

17. At the children's hospital, how does Rosie help Alexander?

Ⓐ She makes sure he takes his medicine.

Ⓑ She plays with him while he has to be alone.

Ⓒ She keeps him company when he is crying.

Ⓓ She helps him eat so that he will get better.

18. At the nursing home, what does Rosie get Bill to do?

Ⓐ laugh   Ⓑ talk

Ⓒ hug   Ⓓ cry

19. What does Rosie's uniform look like?

_____

_____

_____

_____

_____

_____

20. What is the main reason Rosie's owner thinks Rosie is good at her job?

_____

_____

_____

_____

_____

_____

_____

_____

Practice Book
Changing Patterns

Grade 3-I

© Harcourt

The Stories Julian Tells

Directions: For items 1–18, fill in the circle in front of the correct answer. For items 19–20, write the answer.

Vocabulary

1. She could not grab the candy because it was _____ her reach.
  Ⓐ beyond   Ⓑ seriously
  Ⓒ fastened   Ⓓ collection

2. Cora showed Linda how to turn a _____ .
  Ⓐ mustache   Ⓑ collection
  Ⓒ cartwheel   Ⓓ beyond

3. Greg had a white _____ on his lip from drinking milk.
  Ⓐ seriously   Ⓑ mustache
  Ⓒ beyond   Ⓓ fastened

4. Raymond became _____ ill from eating rotten meat.
  Ⓐ seriously   Ⓑ collection
  Ⓒ beyond   Ⓓ patiently

5. Dad _____ his belt tightly so his pants would not fall down.
  Ⓐ collection   Ⓑ beyond
  Ⓒ seriously   Ⓓ fastened

6. My mother has a _____ of pretty tea cups we use when we have company.
  Ⓐ seriously   Ⓑ cartwheel
  Ⓒ fastened   Ⓓ collection

Practice Book
Changing Patterns

Grade 3-1

Comprehension

7. How does Julian change after meeting Gloria?

Ⓐ He doesn't have any friends.

Ⓑ He thinks a girl can be his friend.

Ⓒ He only wants boys for friends.

Ⓓ He starts to play with younger children.

8. How does Julian feel after he falls while trying to turn his first cartwheel?

Ⓐ embarrassed

Ⓑ hurt

Ⓒ mad

Ⓓ okay

9. Gloria tells Julian that it takes practice to turn a cartwheel because she _____ .

Ⓐ is bragging

Ⓑ doesn't want to hurt his feelings

Ⓒ wants to teach him how to do it

Ⓓ is making fun of him

10. How is Gloria's new town different from Newport?

Ⓐ Newport is by the sea, with lots of birds.

Ⓑ There are robins in both Newport and her new town.

Ⓒ Newport is a big city, and her new town is in the country.

Ⓓ Both places are almost exactly alike.

Practice Book
Changing Patterns

11. The mother and father robin do not want Gloria near the nest because they_____ .

   Ⓐ are afraid Gloria will harm the eggs

   Ⓑ don't want Gloria to see their babies

   Ⓒ don't like Gloria

   Ⓓ are afraid Gloria will harm the babies

12. When Julian invites Gloria to his house, he is being _____ .

   Ⓐ bossy   Ⓑ clever

   Ⓒ selfish   Ⓓ friendly

13. What makes Gloria giggle at Julian's house?

   Ⓐ the squawking of the mother robin

   Ⓑ the way the kite looks

   Ⓒ their red mustaches from the Kool-Aid

   Ⓓ the way Julian climbs a tree

14. Why do Julian and Gloria take time to share things with each other?

   Ⓐ Each is looking for a friend.

   Ⓑ They make the same wishes.

   Ⓒ Both are new in the neighborhood.

   Ⓓ Both have younger brothers.

15. Wishes become part of the kite when Julian and Gloria _____ .

   Ⓐ write them on the kite

   Ⓑ tie them in knots to its tail

   Ⓒ glue them to the kite string

   Ⓓ say them as the kite is flying

© Harcourt

Grade 3-1

Practice Book
Changing Patterns

16. What is the kite tail like?

(A) a long white snake

(B) a tired bird

(C) a tiny black spot

(D) banners on the back of a plane

17. Gloria does not tell Julian her wishes because she _____ .

(A) forgets what she wished for

(B) thinks he will laugh

(C) wants her wishes to come true

(D) likes secrets

18. Which word best tells about Gloria?

(A) shy   (B) selfish

(C) proud   (D) serious

19. What do Julian and Gloria use to make their kite?

_____

_____

_____

20. How will Julian and Gloria know if their wishes will come true?

_____

_____

_____

_____

The Talent Show

Directions: For items 1–18, fill in the circle in front of the correct answer. For items 19–20, write the answer.

Vocabulary

1. Every day, we go to the _____ and play basketball.
(A) gym
(B) roam
(C) perform
(D) recite

2. Maria and I will _____ in the school play this year.
(A) prefer
(B) enjoying
(C) perform
(D) roam

3. I _____ chocolate cake for my birthday.
(A) recite
(B) prefer
(C) perform
(D) fastened

4. We are _____ our break from school.
(A) enjoying
(B) perform
(C) prefer
(D) roam

5. Bison used to _____ the Great Plains.
(A) perform
(B) billions
(C) enjoying
(D) roam

6. There are _____ of stars in the sky.
(A) roam
(B) billions
(C) perform
(D) enjoying

7. Christina will _____ the multiplication tables today.
(A) gym
(B) roam
(C) recite
(D) enjoying

Grade 3-1

© Harcourt

Grade 3-1

Comprehension

8. This selection is realistic fiction because _____ .

Ⓐ it takes place in an unreal world

Ⓑ it tells about an event that really happened

Ⓒ the characters and events could have happened

Ⓓ the story took place a long time ago

9. Who is telling this story?

Ⓐ Ms. Babbitt   Ⓑ Beany

Ⓒ Carol Ann   Ⓓ the boys and girls

10. When Ms. Babbitt wears her smiley face earrings, it means _____ .

Ⓐ nothing

Ⓑ that she is happy

Ⓒ that something special will happen

Ⓓ that it is Friday

11. What is Ms. Babbitt's reason for having the talent show?

Ⓐ to have fun   Ⓑ to win a prize

Ⓒ to get a good grade   Ⓓ to perform well

12. What does Carol Ann want to perform with Beany?

Ⓐ a song   Ⓑ a joke

Ⓒ a dance   Ⓓ a poem

Practice Book
Changing Patterns

13. Why does Carol Ann say she should be the "queen bee" in the performance?

Ⓐ She has curly hair.

Ⓑ She has always wanted to be a queen.

Ⓒ Her mother told her she should.

Ⓓ Beany asked her to.

14. Who decides what Carol Ann's and Beany's props and costumes should look like?

Ⓐ Ms. Babbitt   Ⓑ Carol Ann's mom

Ⓒ Beany   Ⓓ Carol Ann

15. What is one reason Beany agrees to perform with Carol Ann?

Ⓐ Beany is a little scared of her.

Ⓑ Carol Ann is her best friend.

Ⓒ Beany knows Ms. Babbitt likes Carol Ann.

Ⓓ Beany wants to.

16. What does Carol Ann think will happen during the performance?

Ⓐ She may forget her lines.

Ⓑ Beany will mess things up.

Ⓒ Ms. Babbitt won't like it.

Ⓓ The class will laugh at them.

17. What does Beany's mother suggest that Beany do for the talent show?

Ⓐ some cartwheels   Ⓑ a different poem

Ⓒ some new songs   Ⓓ a ballet dance

Practice Book
Changing Patterns

18. Beany's dad takes her out to watch the night stars because he wants _____ .

Ⓐ her to count them

Ⓑ to teach her about the planets

Ⓒ her to enjoy them

Ⓓ to see how many constellations she knows

19. In what way does Beany's father compare the night stars to the talent show?

_____

_____

_____

_____

_____

20. What does Beany learn that is important for herself and how she deals with friends?

_____

_____

_____

_____

_____

_____

_____

Practice Book
Changing Patterns

Centerfield Ballhawk

Directions: For items 1–18, fill in the circle in front of the correct answer. For items 19–20, write the answer.

Vocabulary

1. The _____ playing right field caught the ball just before it went over the fence.

   Ⓐ fault   Ⓑ depend

   Ⓒ concentrate   Ⓓ outfielder

2. Jane is called a _____ by her teammates because she is so good at catching balls.

   Ⓐ vanish   Ⓑ ballhawk

   Ⓒ concentrate   Ⓓ fault

3. When I fell on stage, I wished I could just _____ .

   Ⓐ vanish   Ⓑ outfielder

   Ⓒ fault   Ⓓ ballhawk

4. It is not your _____ that we lost the game.

   Ⓐ depend   Ⓑ fault

   Ⓒ ballhawk   Ⓓ concentrate

5. You can always _____ on me to be your friend.

   Ⓐ fault   Ⓑ vanish

   Ⓒ depend   Ⓓ control

6. It is hard to _____ because of all the noise in the room.

   Ⓐ concentrate   Ⓑ gym

   Ⓒ vanish   Ⓓ depend

Grade 3-1

Comprehension

7. Most of the action in this selection takes place _____ .

(A) at the baseball field   (B) in José's front yard

(C) in the new stadium   (D) at the playground

8. Things have been hard for the Mendez family because _____ .

(A) José has been having trouble hitting the ball

(B) Mr. Mendez lost his job

(C) Carmen is a better ballplayer

(D) they haven't gotten over the death of Mrs. Mendez

9. Why is getting more than one hit at the game so important to José?

(A) He thinks it will please his dad.

(B) He's afraid of the coach.

(C) He wants to do better than his sister.

(D) He wants his team to admire him.

10. In this selection a <u>ball</u> is called a _____ .

(A) bat   (B) globe

(C) sphere   (D) circle

11. What is José's first thought when he grounds out?

(A) He thinks his team will be upset.

(B) He is glad his dad isn't there to see him.

(C) He wishes he had practiced more baseball.

(D) He considers quitting baseball.

12. What quick animal is José compared to?

(A) an eagle   (B) a panther

(C) a cheetah   (D) a gazelle

13. What action breaks the tie game?

  Ⓐ A grounder skitters through T.V.'s legs.

  Ⓑ José slams a home run.

  Ⓒ The Bulls strike out.

  Ⓓ José drops the ball.

14. When José asks his teammate "Who's perfect?", what is he thinking of?

  Ⓐ the team's wins and losses

  Ⓑ all of Turtleneck's strikes

  Ⓒ his own batting average

  Ⓓ Ted Jackson's fly balls

15. What does José think will make up for disappointing his dad?

  Ⓐ catching fly balls

  Ⓑ getting a high batting average

  Ⓒ helping the coach

  Ⓓ joining the minors one day

16. What really disappoints José's dad?

  Ⓐ that José has a low batting average

  Ⓑ that José continues to make excuses

  Ⓒ that José skips baseball practice

  Ⓓ that José goes against his dad's wishes

17. What had Carmen been doing that afternoon?

  Ⓐ baking brownies   Ⓑ cheering for José's team

  Ⓒ hitting home runs   Ⓓ baby-sitting

© Harcourt

Practice Book
Changing Patterns

18. José's dad wants José to forget about trying to hit like he did because _____ .

(A) José's strength is as an outfielder

(B) nobody could be as good as he was

(C) José is no good at baseball

(D) he wants José to pitch

19. What does José's dad mean when he says his children are "a chip off the old block"?

_____

_____

_____

_____

_____

20. What is most important to José at the end of the story?

_____

_____

_____

_____

_____

Practice Book
Changing Patterns

Ramona Forever

Directions: For items 1–18, fill in the circle in front of the correct answer. For items 19–20, write the answer.

Vocabulary

1. Max _____ out the window and saw a bird flying by.
- (A) longed
- (B) comfort
- (C) glanced
- (D) unexpected

2. It gives me great _____ when my mother hugs me.
- (A) comfort
- (B) glanced
- (C) contagious
- (D) prescription

3. The doctor told the sick boy to stay home because he might be _____ .
- (A) comfort
- (B) contagious
- (C) glanced
- (D) prescription

4. Dr. Morales wrote a _____ for some medicine for her earache.
- (A) prescription
- (B) longed
- (C) comfort
- (D) glanced

5. During the cold winter, we _____ for summer.
- (A) unexpected
- (B) glanced
- (C) attention
- (D) longed

6. Do not pay any _____ to what they said, because they're wrong.
- (A) comfort
- (B) prescription
- (C) attention
- (D) contagious

7. The surprise party was _____ by my sister.
Ⓐ attention　　　　Ⓑ contagious
Ⓒ unexpected　　　Ⓓ glanced

Comprehension

8. How does Ramona feel about her mother going to the hospital?
Ⓐ worried　　　　Ⓑ pleased
Ⓒ sad　　　　　　Ⓓ angry

9. Right after Mrs. Quimby left for the hospital the girls
decide to _____ .
Ⓐ watch TV
Ⓑ wash the dishes
Ⓒ go to bed
Ⓓ eat the leftover tuna salad

10. This story takes place in _____ .
Ⓐ Alaska　　　　　Ⓑ Florida
Ⓒ Canada　　　　　Ⓓ Oregon

11. What is Mr. Quimby's first name?
Ⓐ Raymond　　　　Ⓑ Hobart
Ⓒ Robert　　　　　Ⓓ Roger

12. The fifth Quimby is _____ .
Ⓐ the new baby　　Ⓑ Ramona
Ⓒ Beezus　　　　　Ⓓ Aunt Bea

Grade 3-I

© Harcourt

Practice Book
Changing Patterns

13. Ramona's heart is pounding at the hospital because she
is _____ .

Ⓐ afraid   Ⓑ hot

Ⓒ tired   Ⓓ excited

14. Why does Ramona feel sick as she waits in the lobby?

Ⓐ The elevator came down much too quickly.

Ⓑ She feels she has the germs that the nurse talked about.

Ⓒ She has a fever.

Ⓓ She has caught germs from the couch.

15. In this story, the word <u>sibling</u> means a _____ .

Ⓐ sore throat   Ⓑ hospital

Ⓒ brother or sister   Ⓓ baby

16. Mr. Quimby gives Ramona a hug and kiss because _____ .

Ⓐ she is very sick

Ⓑ she is brave to wait alone

Ⓒ she needs attention

Ⓓ a woman has scared her

17. Whom does Mrs. Quimby say Roberta looks like?

Ⓐ a picture of a baby on a magazine cover

Ⓑ Ramona when she was a baby

Ⓒ Mr. Quimby when he was a baby

Ⓓ all babies because they all look alike

18. Ramona agrees that she's "wonderful, blunderful" because she is _____ .

Ⓐ playing a word game with Beezus

Ⓑ doing a good job at growing up

Ⓒ learning to calm down her hair

Ⓓ happy her mother is home

19. What beautiful thing does Ramona's mother tell her at the hospital?

_____

_____

_____

_____

_____

_____

20. How is Roberta different from the baby on the cover of *A Name for Your Baby*?

_____

_____

_____

_____

_____

Grade 3-I

© Harcourt

Sayings We Share: Proverbs and Fables

Grade 3-1

Directions: For items 1–18, fill in the circle in front of the correct answer. For items 19–20, write the answer.

Vocabulary

1. My grandmother has very modern ideas for someone from another _____ .
Ⓐ fortunate   Ⓑ summoned
Ⓒ generation   Ⓓ illuminated

2. If you work _____, you will obtain your goal.
Ⓐ generation   Ⓑ fortunate
Ⓒ persistently   Ⓓ summoned

3. The holiday lights _____ the whole town.
Ⓐ illuminated   Ⓑ faithful
Ⓒ fortunate   Ⓓ persistently

4. Mr. Rose came quickly when he was _____ to the office.
Ⓐ faithful   Ⓑ summoned
Ⓒ illuminated   Ⓓ fortunate

5. Kim is an old and _____ friend whom I can always rely on.
Ⓐ generation   Ⓑ faithful
Ⓒ summoned   Ⓓ persistently

6. We are _____ that we have good health.
Ⓐ fortunate   Ⓑ summoned
Ⓒ faithful   Ⓓ generation

Comprehension

7. According to the selection, you learn much about life
from _____ .

Ⓐ characters in books   Ⓑ brothers and sisters

Ⓒ older family members   Ⓓ teachers and coaches

8. Another name for "common sayings" is _____ .

Ⓐ proverbs   Ⓑ rhymes

Ⓒ fables   Ⓓ fairy tales

9. Oral traditions are usually stories or sayings that different
cultures _____ .

Ⓐ use to teach their young about art

Ⓑ say each year at holiday time

Ⓒ require the young to memorize

Ⓓ pass down from generation to generation

10. Proverbs from around the world may use different words, but
many of the _____ are the same.

Ⓐ ideas   Ⓑ locations

Ⓒ sentences   Ⓓ stories

11. Which American saying is similar to the Vietnamese saying
"Even with two hands, one cannot catch two fish at one time"?

Ⓐ Silence is golden.

Ⓑ One today is worth a thousand tomorrows.

Ⓒ Don't spread yourself too thin.

Ⓓ As a crab walks, so walks its children.

Practice Book
Changing Patterns

Grade 3-1

© Harcourt

12. The moral of a story is the _____ that the story teaches.

  Ⓐ generation   Ⓑ expression

  Ⓒ lesson   Ⓓ tradition

13. Arnold Lobel uses the tale of the rooster to teach that in order to succeed, you _____ .

  Ⓐ may fail at first   Ⓑ must yell loudly

  Ⓒ must be grown up   Ⓓ need sunshine

14. What is the meaning of "he who lays down with dogs shall rise up with fleas"?

  Ⓐ A sleeping cat cannot catch the rat.

  Ⓑ A person is known by the company he keeps.

  Ⓒ The dogs are looking for their pet fleas.

  Ⓓ It is difficult to raise a family of fleas.

15. The lazy mouse goes hungry because she _____ .

  Ⓐ doesn't understand how to gather beans

  Ⓑ didn't run for help in time

  Ⓒ played when she should have worked

  Ⓓ had a hard time finding snakeskin at night

16. "Slow and steady wins the race" is the moral for the fable _____ .

  Ⓐ "The Hare and the Tortoise"

  Ⓑ "American Fable"

  Ⓒ "French Fable"

  Ⓓ "Two Mice"

17. Aesop's fables were written _____ .

  Ⓐ in present times   Ⓑ over 2,000 years ago

  Ⓒ about the future   Ⓓ in Spanish

Grade 3-1

Practice Book
Changing Patterns

18. This selection is most like a _____ .

Ⓐ journal entry   Ⓑ magazine article

Ⓒ news story   Ⓓ biography

19. How are fables and proverbs alike?

_____

_____

_____

_____

_____

_____

_____

20. How are the dog and the wolf in the French fable different?

_____

_____

_____

_____

_____

_____

_____

_____